A CLOSING CULTURE

[illegible],
Keep closing it!

A CLOSING Culture

Your MARKETING *and* SALES PROCESS *is* BROKEN. HERE'S HOW *to* FIX IT

JOSH HARCUS

A CLOSING CULTURE
Your Marketing and Sales Process Is Broken.
Here's How to Fix It

ISBN 978-1-61961-453-6 *Paperback*
978-1-61961-454-3 *Ebook*

LIONCREST
PUBLISHING

To all the frustrated salespeople who
know that the game has changed,
but their company has not.

CONTENTS

ACKNOWLEDGMENTS

THANK YOU:

Allie Hoffman for all of your hard work in keeping us organized and on top of all the moving parts with this book. Kyle Kramer for the late night (and early morning) discussions around the sales processes detailed in later chapters. John Gelardi for your camaraderie and continuous support. Jim Kittridge for being such a good friend and challenging my ideas until they are perfected or killed. George Taylor for pushing me to start Hüify during my days of uncertainty. My Edge mentorship group for your weekly words of wisdom. Tom Eggleston for your enthusiasm and delight with my work. Erika Harcus for your admiration of me as your older brother. Mom for your excitement around this endeavour. Dad for your pride in me and the passions that I have been given. And lastly the most beautiful mind (and more) that I have ever known, my wonderful wife, Sara Rose Harcus. I truly could not have done this book without your help. From late night revising to your continual kind works of inspiration, you are such a marvelous woman.

FOREWORD

You are about to begin a white water rafting trip with Josh so let me point out what to watch for.

Creativity: Josh grew up as a street performer not because his family was homeless but because he could mesmerize an audience that was present by accident.

Think of it, you want to get to work, or home, or to lunch, or to a meeting, and you walk upon a magician who is brilliant and draws you in by his banter and skill.

He can encounter hecklers and distractions, each one of which is incorporated into the improv of the performance, just like there is no perfect script for your company.

Do you have the wisdom and insight to respond to the market dynamics? Beware the bear: Josh loves extreme sports, surfing treacherous waves, para-sailing in hurricane winds, mountain biking in the Rockies leaping over canyons and critters. Josh has no fear, even of a 12′ grizzly, so he is be bold in his ideas, pushing his clients to reinvent their business or at the least to reinvent how they think about their customers.

Data-centric: Josh is less good with feelings that he is with facts, more interested in data than in opinions, so a plan he builds must be measurable and insure the measures track how do you achieve sustainable growth through real value.

White water rapids: A new competitor, a dazzling new technology can send your company for a spin, like loss of control in a level 5 rapids. The rocks and undertow can be overwhelming. Josh is in your stern using his paddle skillfully to call each rock by name he is so familiar with the dangers.

Custom-made: As you read you will insert your circumstances and find the examples and illustrations to draw out your Customer-centric solution like it was custom-made for you.

Know the GAP: Josh is co-founder and CEO of Hüify, ranked by HubSpot one of the top three inbound marketing firms in the US. Rather than solve the tricky transition to inbound marketing for clients alone, Josh unlocks the revenue of a relationship with long-term, delighted Customers. The GAP between inbound marketing and sales is the waterfall journey Josh will lead you on. Few can beat the odds so listen well.

Rowers: Your boat is full of your team for this is a journey to create the culture of instant response with relevant and compelling responses to the prospect's trepidations. Two great rowers on the port side will only cause the boat to spin in circles. Everyone needs to pull in synchrony to Josh your coxswain. You are in for an adventure, a dinner of fresh fish caught in the white water grilled over your fire with no flint to start it, served on Josh's paddle that steers you.

A feast awaits.

TOM EGGLESTON

CEO, RENU Management

Managing Director, Charmides Capital

INTRODUCTION

It all started with Ellie.

Aided by naturally flowing hand gestures and a caring, approachable demeanor, a smart, short-haired woman named Ellie Mirman (@ellieeille) took the stage in a room filled with five hundred marketing experts and told them the way they'd been doing things was all wrong. It was the fall of 2011, years before "content marketing" became the signature buzzword of the industry, and this young marketer was urging executives twice her age to change not only their approach to marketing but also, in some cases, their entire business model.

At the time, Ellie and I were both speakers at a conference circuit called CrushIQ, alongside representatives from several industry heavyweights: Google, Facebook, Bing, and HubSpot.

At this time, I had experienced the results of inbound marketing with my own companies and would preach its principles when prompted. I had grown accustomed to clients favoring its approach but claiming they simply didn't have the time to implement it.

I watched from afar as Ellie's impeccably executed speech received a similar response. The audience nodded in agreement with every point she made: they wanted to provide content on their websites to attract visitors, convert those visitors who were interested in what they were selling into leads, and then put those leads in touch with a salesperson who could close the deal. During a question-and-answer session at the conclusion of her presentation, nearly every person in the room wondered, "Who's going to do all of this?"

She told them, "You're going to do all of this."

In reality, they weren't. The men and women in that room already had their plates full with work and certainly didn't have the time—or, in some cases, the ability—to crank out blog posts at the rate needed to make the approach successful. What if someone could do it for them and in the process help those businesses grow really quickly?

With that question still weighing on my mind, I left to host a breakout session critiquing websites, and that's where I met Andy, a short, fiery bald man with a natural talent for team building that was evident as soon as he introduced himself. In those days, Andy was the director of marketing for a heavy equipment rental company whose products were the primary offerings in that category at Home Depots across the country.

Andy's duties weren't limited to marketing in the traditional sense: he also made sure the company's channels and stores were operating correctly. He knew writing blog posts and providing information online were necessary tasks, but he was also keenly aware that he wouldn't be able to handle them on his own given his myriad of other responsibilities. As an alternative, he considered hiring a full-time content creator, but feared that person would eventually end up performing some of his work at the expense of the duties he would have originally hired him or her for.

After elaborating on these challenges, he finally asked me, "What would it take for your company to bring us on as a client partner and start to do that stuff for us?"

That was the genesis of Hüify (pronounced Hue-ify; @TeamHuify). Four short years later, Hüify became one of HubSpot's top customer-reviewed agency partners, ranking higher than three thousand other companies spread across sixty-five countries. And while we view certainly the designation as an honor, we're also keenly aware that operating in that echelon of excellence raises the expectations of the prospects with whom we will do business. It's imperative that every decision be made correctly, and with a level of foresight that precludes actions which might set our partners up for any degree of failure. By striving to meet and exceed those standards, we force ourselves to become better at what we do on a daily basis.

It was through these unyielding efforts to improve that we came to advocate a more comprehensive application of the inbound philosophy for both marketing and sales efforts—one that treats it as a complete methodology rather than a practice or a specific set of deliverables. Adopting that mindset meant resisting the urge to produce content for content's sake and directing our energies toward creating sales activity that would drive results measured by the only metric that matters: revenue.

In the process, we discovered the most effective way to achieve our goal was to wed three aspects of marketing that are often viewed as disparate—or even competing—areas of focus.

First, we needed to fulfill the fundamental purpose of content marketing by producing work written to educate and ultimately convert leads. After all, a marketing strategy that lacks the capacity to attract and retain prospective customers simply isn't much of a strategy, and failing in such a critical way would have doomed our efforts before they ever began.

At the same time, it's nearly impossible to judge exactly what constitutes great work if what's produced is measured solely by the instincts and preferences of the people involved in creating it. Even if those intuitive metrics turn out to be correct, they leave little room for the kind of feedback that might make a good strategy even more effective. Thus the second component to our methodology became rooted in fostering a culture of continual testing and refining messages based on all the available data.

But facilitating the collection of that data and fostering the tools needed to act on it would be a Herculean feat for even the most talented team of marketers without the aid of technology. That's what made our partnership with HubSpot the final, and perhaps most vital, piece of the strategic jigsaw puzzle we were assembling. We recognized early on that success would require us to remain experts in the ever-evolving world of customer relationship management software. That focus ultimately evolved to such a degree that we became innovators, combining different tools in previously unexpected ways to better serve our goal. Today, HubSpot is rolling out some of the very systems we created to its other partner agencies.

PARTNERS > VENDORS

As we went about implementing this methodology with our clients, it quickly became apparent that doing so would require a great deal of trust on their part. And why wouldn't it? Fully embracing the process would mean turning control of their entire marketing strategy over to us, whereas most agencies operated more like vendors than genuine partners.

So what's the difference? A great vendor can take a laundry list of items from a client, check them off by a certain deadline, and receive a top review. A great partner, meanwhile, will take the time to truly understand a business and push back against some items on that list if they aren't likely to yield the best return.

When we do push back, our clients are able to drill any member of our team with questions about why things are being done a certain way, and each Hüify team member will provide an articulate answer, detailing everything from what the impact of a given task will be to the consequences of inaction.

What truly sets our method apart is the ability to see problems in strategy or practice before they arise and address them before they cause greater issues. This contrast is most obvious when dealing with clients' initial requests. For example, a client's first instinct is to ask an agency for a new website, but when asked the reason why, no one can explain the rationale behind that so-called need.

A vendor in this situation might respond with a plan for a new website and a projection of cost, all without ever looking at measurable data to determine if it's actually in the client's best interest. Because we view the relationship with our clients as a long-term arrangement rather than a short-term opportunity to increase our revenue, we might recommend against that $40,000 website project unless the data proves it's absolutely necessary.

That may sound unrealistically altruistic, but the fact is, our process demands that we only focus our energy on that which is most likely to help clients achieve their goals. When they do, we know that rising tide will lift our ship alongside theirs, and thus we have grown comfortable with sacrificing in the short term so that we can both prosper later.

Decisions like that do more than save our clients money. In some cases, they can save entire businesses. There are countless examples of e-commerce sites with sales that plummeted after launching a new website purely because they wanted something "new and fresh." In the '90s, it was sports retailer Boo.com, which began its collapse with an ultra-complicated redesign just prior to the dot-com boom. Last year, it was Marks & Spencer, whose online sales plummeted by over 8 percent in the first quarter due to a redesign that DigitasLBi (@Digitas) marketer Ed Beard said makes it unclear whether their site "is a magazine or somewhere to buy a shirt."

In both cases, and in hundreds of others, companies not only spent untold hours and dollars putting their new sites together but also actually harmed their businesses instead of creating a return by launching them. All of that could have been avoided with some simple analytics, which is why we consider analysis of data vital to what we do.

Of course, it's not always the misguided desire for a new website that we have to contend with. Often it's something as simple as overly vague goals that need to be refined before we can put our method into practice.

This typically manifests itself in the form of a request for additional leads, but a lead, by definition, is nothing more than a person or company's contact information. Any agency can run a free iPad giveaway on its website and generate tons of "leads," but they wouldn't be qualified or even valuable in terms of driving revenue.

We wanted our method to be different, so we built it around conducting an analysis of the revenue each lead could generate if they became a customer (customer lifetime value, CLTV for short) and then comparing that to our clients' goals. With the current close rate, how many leads would we need to generate to achieve a certain revenue goal? Once that question is answered, the real work begins in the form of developing a strategic plan to reach those goals. Then we provide the tools to help our clients stay the course, even after we're no longer part of the picture.

We recognized early on that the key to success for both our agency and our clients lies in developing a deeper understanding of their goals. Sometimes those goals are as simple as looking awesome in front of their bosses.

Remember Andy, the equipment rental marketer who started this whole thing? He knew he couldn't do everything by himself, but by bringing in someone who could, he still received credit for the work the agency produced because he was the one who convinced the company's leadership that hiring us was a good decision.

At the end of the day, relationships like that come down

to trust, which means another primary function of our method is to develop a "best judgment" culture where no one is seeking to control every aspect of the process. It seems every single person in the world has an opinion on the way something should be marketed and few will be willing to hand control of that process over to an expert, even if he or she is the one who hired the expert in the first place.

It goes without saying that having someone constantly challenge the process is going to impede progress, even if the person is smart and good at what he or she does. That person will force the reselling of concepts at every turn, or worse, expect a return on the marketing investment almost immediately, regardless of whether the sales cycle is three months or a year long.

That's like hiring a contractor to build a house and then wondering why it doesn't look like the concept sketches when he's barely poured the foundation. If you pepper him with questions to that effect every time he drives a nail, it's going to take a very long time to build your home—that is, if he doesn't quit long before the project is concluded.

Why would he quit? Because he knows it's silly to hire experts and then act as if you know what's best.

Building a new marketing strategy works much the same way, and it's vital to the success of a given engagement that clients trust us and their in-house marketers to use our best judgment. When they do, we all can do amazing things together and make the process practical, efficient, and, ultimately, beneficial for everyone involved. That doesn't mean things won't break down along the way (we are still working with human beings, after all), but it does mean that everyone involved can recognize those challenges as a part of the process that provides an opportunity to improve rather than viewing them as failures.

At Hüify, we're fortunate to have had clients who bought into that concept, and we are grateful that they have reviewed us so highly, but this book isn't really about us. It isn't about me. In fact, it isn't even about inbound marketing. There are already excellent books on marketing and selling, such as *Inbound Marketing* by Brian Halligan (@bhalligan) and Dharmesh Shah (@dharmesh), or *Baseline Selling* by Dave Kurlan (@KurlanAssoc). This book is nestled between those two—it's not about marketing tactics, and it's not about sales tactics.

Instead, this book exists to address a single fundamental and near-universal flaw we've discovered in otherwise great companies, large and small, across the globe: a breakdown in communication and collaboration between salespeople and marketers we refer to as the Gap.

The Gap manifests itself in different ways, ranging from the painfully obvious to the subtle and insidious. Sometimes, the two departments are housed in entirely separate buildings or even states, which turns our metaphorical problem into a literal, physical one. In less extreme cases, there are other clues: leads are brought in who don't match the company's target demographic, while those with every indication that they're the type of customers the company hopes to attract aren't closed.

To address these issues, the key players in each department have to know when to switch hats between attracting leads (marketing) and closing those leads (selling), drive more conversions, and connect people with where they need to go. In other words, the two departments must work cohesively, bridge the Gap between them, and recognize a fundamental truth: they're striving for the same goal, and achieving it will happen more efficiently if they work together.

We've found that this laser-like focus on goals allows the people involved to release the emotional ties to their individual ideas and concentrate on proven methods and actions. Once staff members are operating under that mindset, they're free to break things, discover things, and stretch things to their limits, often leading to some truly magical successes because they are using their best judgment based on all the available data.

This creates an environment free of the bureaucratic system of constant checks and balances that often stands in the way of employees taking small, calculated risks with the potential for big payouts. In its place, we build a system that rewards and encourages innovation because all of the people involved know they're being judged solely on the overall success of the project.

An unintended but beneficial side-effect of that culture is that the motivation of the people involved is no longer solely dependent on the need to maintain a steady paycheck or avoid being fired. Offering employees the opportunity to make small gambles on their ideas fosters a sense of accomplishment that money alone never could, and taps into the intrinsic motivation inherent to all human beings.

And why wouldn't it? Innovation is fun and exciting, particularly for someone who had a stake in bringing it to fruition. Empowering employees to take chances not only makes that growth more likely to occur, but gives them a measure of personal enjoyment in seeing the eventual outcome.

If that sounds like the kind of culture you'd like to see put in place at your company, look no further. The tools and processes described in this book are designed to do exactly that while simultaneously increasing leads, conversions, and revenue. By its conclusion, you'll have all the information you need to set effective goals, make them a reality, and sustain that success for years to come.

CHAPTER 1

SETTING YOUR GOALS

Above all else, the Gap is the result of a fundamental misconception about why certain customers do business with certain companies. Depending on your perspective, you might be suffering from any number of illusions that contribute to the problem.

Sales directors will often complain that marketing doesn't help their department bring in qualified leads and inhibits them from closing more deals. They operate on the belief that the power to do so lies solely in the hands of salespeople, and their ability to talk prospects into a deal. They may think that all they need to close more deals is more leads, and while that may be true to a certain extent, that line of thinking fails to account for the greater percentage of deals they might close if those leads were better primed to make a purchase.

Marketers sometimes err in a similar way, assuming that all they need to do is fill the pipeline with leads, regardless of quality or the degree of interest indicated by the leads themselves. They may even believe they're doing their jobs well simply by building awareness about their company, but the truth is people don't go online to research companies. They research problems.

It's no secret we live in an age of unprecedented information sharing, and accessibility to limitless knowledge on the Internet has put all of the power in the hands of the buyer. No one has to listen to a salesperson's pitch and believe every word—you can literally fact-check them in real time with a few taps on a smartphone.

There was a time when the most aggressive salespeople always put up the biggest numbers, but since the Internet fundamentally changed the way buyers shop for products, the market has evolved into an environment that favors the smart over the bold. Customers are more educated than ever, and although that means they are better informed about the potential solutions your product can offer, they're also increasingly aware of the possible problems it could cause. They're going to ask tough questions, and all the smooth talkers in the world won't be able to top a sales team well versed in problem solving.

Done properly, marketing can educate customers about those solutions before they ever speak to a salesperson and ideally move the lead from the "awareness stage" of the buyer's journey toward the "consideration stage" before any discussion with a salesperson has to happen at all. By the time it does, the customer has usually already decided to buy (decision stage). The salesperson just needs to get him or her past the initial hesitation to act on that decision.

With that in mind, it seems obvious that sales and marketing are invaluable to one another, but because of these lingering misconceptions, there is often friction between the two departments. Marketing tends to value quantity over quality, and sales knows that without quality, all the quantity in the world is useless. It's typical for both to compound the problem by operating on the same misguided philosophy: that their company or product, not their solution to the customer's problem, is what's ultimately going to help them make a sale. The relationship between marketing and sales is like a fishing vessel and fishermen; the fishermen can do an excellent job catching fish from the shore, but they will get nowhere near the quality or quantity they could catch if they worked from a fishing vessel that sets out to a sea voyage.

As CEO of Hüify, I've seen it happen firsthand while working with businesses such as the equipment rental company

I mentioned earlier. They were so focused on building awareness for their products that they did not take into account the specific needs that would drive people to seek them out. After all, there aren't many people who care about different models of skid steers, but there are thousands of people who spend weekends trying to build their own pergolas or installing a French drain. So, that is what we did. We answered simple questions for company's future customers (e.g., How do I build a privacy fence?), and once we reached them by providing the answers they were looking for, they were more likely to close into a sale.

The same could be said for a software company we worked with. Their focus on the array of features their products offered prevented them from taking advantage of obvious opportunities to solve their customers' problems. There are comparable examples, many of which are detailed in this book, that illustrate the new world today's marketing and sales professionals are navigating. Stop focusing on you solutions and instead focus on your customers' problem.

Developing a sales team that performs well in this environment requires a cultural change that emphasizes close attention to the individual needs of each lead in each business. What questions are your prospects seeking answers to? What matters to them? What are their stories? What is going to make them look good internally? What goals do they have? The ability to answer these questions is paramount to the success or failure of any given sales engagement, and the people best positioned to provide those answers are the marketers who cultivated the lead in the first place.

Too many times, though, the Gap comes between them: sales is responsible for a certain set of metrics, marketing is responsible for a different set, and no one in the equation realizes that these two entities should be working so closely together that they almost seem to be one and the same. These situations beg for an alignment where both parties are codependent on one another and celebrate each other's successes.

At face value, such an alignment may seem obvious, but too often fear and ignorance lead people to continue doing things the way they've always been done them. When a system yields at least some positive results, as even these old-fashioned ones tend to do, it's easy to overlook their inherent inefficiency. In fact, the people involved may not even realize the plethora of opportunities they're passing up just because they're too afraid of "fixing what isn't broken." They do not understand that operating at 20 percent efficiency does mean the system is broken. However, they will when they see their margins decreasing while their costs per customer rise. To bring back in our fishing vessel analogy, think of a fishing trawler. These ships drag a huge net under water with the goal of catching a ton of anchovies, shrimp, tuna, and mackerel. A sales and marketing department moving forward without alignment is like the fishing crew deciding to go back out into the sea while they have huge gaping holes in their net, but because they are still catching a few fish, they decide to press on with their voyage. The cost per new customer (fish) is significantly high when salaries, supplies, fuel, and engine repairs are taken into account, but often this matter is attributed to the status of the "industry" or the "current economy" instead of focusing on the gaping holes in the process.

Consider the Hüify method a humble attempt at suggesting something better: a cultural shift where both sales and marketing see each other as needed departments; where the focus isn't on what each department is doing individually, but what's being accomplished cooperatively; and where both are doing all they can to help each other grow.

The first step to creating this synergistic system is to establish a clearly defined set of goals around which the two departments (and the company as a whole) can rally and progress can be tracked. At their core, the goals have to be focused on achieving growth as measured by revenue. Instead of measuring deals like a race that is won or lost, companies need to analyze each lap. If you promise to define these goals according to revenue, I promise to not use the word synergistic for the rest of this book.

For many organizations, it will be tempting to communicate these goals as deliverables: a certain number of blog posts, a selection of ebooks, or even name badges for different conferences. Surprisingly, that's what a lot of marketing people are doing, usually in the absence of any data that proves these activities help the company capture and convert leads.

Instead, they should be talking about their goals on an existential level, for example, how much additional revenue they need to open a new office, acquire a competitor, or, in the case of early stage companies, raise additional funding. While many CEOs would opt to keep these goals broad and vague, we've found the process works best when they are at least as refined and specific as the aforementioned examples.

After all, if a company's stated goal is simply "to gain customers," their employees and partners might choose to accept the addition of a single customer as success. It goes without saying that that probably isn't what the CEO had in mind, which is why it's important to determine exactly what changes are to be expected and what significant milestones the company will see on its path to achieving them. In other words, a goal should be specific, measurable, attainable, relevant, and timely—SMART.

Any goal that doesn't meet this criteria opens the door to miscommunication and disappointment, because the concepts being discussed can have different interpretations for the parties involved. If a client thinks "more customers" means one hundred new customers and an agency thinks it means fifty, it's not hard to see how the differing perceptions are likely to lead to future turmoil. A SMART goal, by contrast, lays out clear guidelines: eight new customers by December 31 or $500,000 in new revenue by August 15.

Developing these kind of goals is so logical that efforts to do so rarely ever face resistance other than in cases where those specific goals have simply never been set or where a person's pride interferes with his or her ability to think critically. Marketing managers, in particular, don't want to seem like they don't know how to do their job and can't exactly question their bosses about knowledge they should have had all along but only just realized they were lacking. The funny reality is, their bosses may not know the answers either, so everyone ends up espousing a generic need for more customers in order to avoid appearing incompetent.

The result of such vague instructions is similar to that of a ship captain who simply commands his crew to sail without providing details about their destination beyond the general direction in which it might be located. Unable to accurately determine the supplies they'll need for the journey, the size vessel required, or whether they need to recruit more sailors to aid in their quest, the shipmates are bound to become frustrated as each operates on his own interpretation of the ultimate goal. The ensuing dischord might prevent the expedition from achieving its purpose entirely, but even if it doesn't, odds are the voyage will require more time and resources than it might have if it had been properly planned. Once that comes to light, you can bet the crew will be entertaining some mutinous thoughts—if they remain on board the ship at all.

Captains of industry rarely need to worry about being violently overthrown, but the sad reality remains that most organizations don't have SMART goals, and the most common reason is that it's easier for the people leading them to pretend the status quo is acceptable—even if they're secretly terrified of navigating the unfamiliar waters of their evolving business. When someone questions that status quo, there's a temptation for the person in charge to offer a bullish response because it can feel like he or she is being called out.

So how does one go about circumventing these insecurities when starting the conversations needed to develop his or her company's SMART goals? One way is to have the discussion outside of a workplace environment, where the individual in charge feels less of a compulsion to put on the front that's preventing the company from moving forward. Perhaps more importantly, taking your superior to a one-on-one lunch or dinner demonstrates that you care about him or her, and you are committed to driving your superior's success, not planning some crazy mutiny or mass exodus from the company.

Getting people into a different environment, even for a short time, often tricks the brain into building a deeper relationship with the person who's sharing that new environment with you. After all, nothing fosters a more rock-solid bond than shared memories, and visiting new places together is a foolproof way to create some.

The majority of conversations you have with your boss probably take place in fewer than ten rooms, but if you expand that to, say, fifty rooms over the course of a few months, you build a closer bond that demonstrates commitment. Once there's a strong connection in place, you can ask the kind of leading questions that are likely to help your boss formulate answers that he or she might not have previously considered.

I found myself in a similar situation during a recent conversation with a gentleman who had developed software that analyzes a person's golf game. Designed to help players understand how they approach the sport mentally and ultimately improve their abilities, the tool helps to calm the mind and allows golfers to perform at the peak of their skill level.

That may sound like a creation with a lot of potential for expansion and monetization, but it was clear from the beginning that its creator didn't know where he wanted to take the product next. Much like the otherwise successful CEOs operating without clearly defined goals, our inventor couldn't create a plan because he didn't have a specific endgame in mind for his product.

The best way to help someone past such hurdles is to start asking personal questions: What is your goal for this? What do you want out of it? Personally, where do you want to go?

Eventually, the personal goals shared in the answers to these kinds of questions will allude to professional ones. From there, you can begin to tailor your questions so that they suggest the specific milestones that will lead to the realization of those goals. If your boss admits he'd like to open a second office, for example, you need to know the amount of extra revenue it will take to make that happen. With that in mind, it's a simple matter of using his answers to build the blocks of what the goal should be and then shaping those blocks around the previously discussed personal goals.

Does this sound complicated? It doesn't have to be. In fact, the conversation might go like this:

YOU: "We want to open another office. Who would I need to talk to in order to figure out the amount of revenue we would need to open that office?"

BOSS: "Actually, I have all that information right here. It would take around five hundred thousand dollars, but it means changes x, y, and z must also take place."

YOU: "OK, so based on those numbers, it looks like we need to do $1.6 million in sales if we factor in our insurance to be able to hit that number and open up the next office. Is that what you're telling me?"

BOSS: "Yeah, that sounds exactly right."

YOU: "Awesome. I'm trying to rally my team. I've been having a hard time, but it seems you just gave me the perfect goal. Is this the goal you want us to push toward?"

BOSS: "Yes, this is exactly the goal I want you to push toward."

YOU: "Can I build a plan based on the goal of opening up a new office by reaching $1.6 million in revenue?"

BOSS: "That would be great. It's a smart move, and I really appreciate your initiative. Here's one million dollars for your efforts."

OK, so not the last part. You get the idea, though.

By addressing your superiors in this manner, you can succeed in pushing them forward as leaders without seeming threatening. At the same time, you'll acquire the kind of crystal-clear goal you were seeking in the first place.

Goals that well defined are so rare in the business world, they may as well be unicorns, and when people finally have one, it's shocking how quickly they will rally around a common purpose. This, in turn, goes a long way toward creating a result-driven culture, where employees can work whenever and do whatever they want as long as they hit their goals.

It's this kind of environment that fuels companies such as WordPress, where over two hundred employees work virtually from locations all across the globe. A company can implement such a successful operation only after it has taken the time to establish what it means to achieve its goals and what it means to show results. Once that's done, all staff members will have the ability to make a difference in the organization by using their intrinsic intelligence to figure out solutions that get the organization closer to its revenue target.

Often, there is a trickle-down effect where even development-level employees will alter their workflow to pursue the goal. Instead of simply churning out release after release, they can look past the amount of work in front of them and view things critically, prioritizing that which is most likely to push the company toward completion of its grand vision. As we will cover in more depth later, this kind of culture allows team members to focus their energies on what's going to provide the most value to the customers with whom the organization most wants to do business and to shift release dates as needed to pursue the company's ultimate revenue target.

In other words, they can adopt a growth-driven, decision-making process that not only shreds red tape in favor of results but also promotes the same type of intrinsic motivation discussed back in the introduction of this book. It can be incredibly empowering to know that every extra hour worked or new idea crafted is pushing the company toward its ultimate goal, whether that effort comes in the form of putting together a better invoicing system or figuring out a better template for blogging.

With their motivation no longer focused on working harder to avoid getting fired, the focus for team members shifts to playing a role in achieving something bigger than themselves.

CHAPTER 2

IDENTIFYING YOUR CUSTOMERS

Once a mindset of intrinsic motivation is in place, it's time for the major players in the organization to begin formulating a plan to achieve their SMART goal. The first step is identifying what kind of customers are going to help them get there.

Without the aid of a crystal ball that predicts the future, this can seem like a challenging endeavor when taken at face value. After all, how can a company possibly hope to predict where its customers will come from and what they'll be like when they only just figured out what their goals are?

Interestingly enough, the answer usually comes from a

cursory review of the organization's existing clients. Who is bringing in the most money? Who is easiest to work with? Start with that person and break down what exactly makes that client tick until you have the characteristics distilled to a specific image: your ideal client, right now.

We refer to this hypothetical client as a buyer persona—a snapshot of the type of customer most likely to help the company grow as quickly as possible. Obviously, this profile will be radically different for different businesses, but the principal questions involved in crafting the buyer persona are always the same.

We once worked with a channel relationship management software company. Their main focus was connecting with a client company's head of sales—someone in their late thirties with ambition to grow and a desire to make their process better. They discovered that this ideal client works in a corporate environment, and even though their job is a typical Monday–Friday 9–5, it wouldn't be out of the ordinary to catch them researching work-related information on the weekend because they love their career. In fact, the highest traffic-generating days of the week are Friday and Saturday for some of our B2B clients' content.

Possessing this kind of in-depth knowledge about potential clients' likely behavior allowed the company to create a strategy tailor-made to reel them in. Rather than trying to close deals with only their intuition to guide them, their salespeople now knew the ideal time frame in which to contact their leads, what their leads personal lives might look like, and what drives them in their careers.

It wasn't long before the effect of all this knowledge extended well beyond the realm of sales and marketing. Being aware that your customers are likely to work on weekends, for example, means you also know you need 24-7 customer support so that any potential issues can be addressed immediately.

That kind of thinking causes a company to slowly build its long-term strategies around its clients' needs and values. Then its service and product naturally conform to the skeleton of that strategy—all of which can only be attained with the invaluable insights of the firm's buyer personas.

Once a handful of those personas have been crafted and ranked according to the amount of revenue they are likely to generate, executives in the organization can more accurately communicate to their staff who these customers truly are and, more importantly, who they aren't. Possessing these details all but eliminates the possibility of miscommunication between marketing and sales, because marketing now knows the difference between a lead and a qualified lead—knowledge that allows them to instruct the sales team as to which leads are more likely to yield valuable results.

Remember, marketers are usually more familiar with their company's website than the sales staff because they were likely involved in its construction. This puts them in an ideal position to analyze and break down the flow of leads and to truly understand why those leads interacted with a certain feature on the site itself. Forwarding that information to sales primes that department to prioritize their time and offer instant response to the most promising leads rather than doing all of that research themselves, increasing the efficiency with which they can approach and close leads.

Better yet, the automation of this information forwarding makes the process even more seamless. For example, say marketing identifies that people who return to the pricing page two or more times end up converting at 3x the rate of leads who never visit this page at all. The marketing team can then set up a notification to let the salesperson know when that a lead has viewed the pricing page two times. Now, that salesperson can identify and invest their time is these primed leads who keep coming back to the pricing page. That salesperson can even go as far as to call that person in real time, because these notifications let them know when that lead is viewing the page. Creepy, right? But insanely effective.

Collaborating in this manner goes a long way toward strengthening the alliance between the two teams because everyone's collective effort is focused on the same goal, as opposed to the likely alternative that individual ideas wind up competing against one another.

Failing to follow this process complicates things immensely because people end up operating on misconceptions, particularly about where traffic goes. It's often assumed, for example, that 90 percent of web traffic lands on a company's homepage first, but in reality, this is hardly ever the case for high-converting websites. It is likely that only a third of your visitors are coming in through the homepage—this has been observed in almost every traffic analysis we've ever performed. Most of your visitors will not experience the homepage as the first page they see.

That means the remaining two thirds of a company's hits originate from a blog post, about page, or another one of your website's hundred plus indexed pages. That fact alone should make it painfully obvious where companies need to focus their attention, but there remains an overwhelming and ubiquitous fixation on homepages that just doesn't make any sense. In fact, it often seems companies want their homepage to be a flawless document that communicates every single thing about their organization, and they make matters worse by trying to do it with some ridiculous “voice” or “brand” that supposedly makes it unique among the myriad of other content on the Internet.

Then there are those who argue their buyer persona is built around some unique individual who “doesn’t read blogs.” The irony of this contention is that almost any page on any website could be classified as a piece of content that is equivalent to a blog post, meaning any person who consumes information online is almost certainly reading them. They may not admit it—or even consciously realize it—but that doesn’t change the fact that it’s true.

Marketers inherently recognize the foolishness of these erroneous ideas because they observe the flow of web traffic on a daily basis, which makes it vital that they have a voice in determining which parts of a company’s website receive the most attention. Providing them with that platform will not only suppress the temptation to overthink an organization’s homepage, but it will also stave off another misconception that often arises from poor communication: the idea that a top-down approach where articles are filtered through the communicative faculties of the company’s upper management is necessary or valuable.

This typically arises when the executives in question object to the tone or voice of a given blog post or other document. "I would never write the article that way," they'll often argue, as if it's in any way possible for another person to compose the piece in a way that expresses his or her boss's unique personality. The fact is, it isn't possible, and even if it were, it wouldn't be any more likely to affect sales than possessing the perfect homepage.

Remember, customers aren't coming to a company's website because they enjoy the voice in which the information there is presented. They're visiting because they think the information itself might help them solve a problem, and executives need to remember that sharing that information in a way that spurs people to make purchases is why they hired a marketing team in the first place.

The only alternative is for them to write articles themselves, which isn't something that should be in the job description of a CEO, if for no other reason than the absurd cost of their time. Unless a company wants articles that approach $1,000–$2,000 per post, the people in charge must necessarily be persuaded to avoid acting on opinions lodged in the way they feel or think. Instead, they should let the professionals they've selected do what data suggests is effective.

After all, ideas are cheap. If you and I sat down together, we could probably come up with fifty ideas for new companies in a twenty-minute time span, and a lot of them would probably be great. However, dreaming up ideas costs us nothing, but execution, on the other hand, is costly. All ideas must be filtered with growth-driven data and ranked by priority and impact.

Failing to follow that simple edict can have serious effects on an organization's bottom line. Remember the equipment rental company from earlier? Before working with us, they were convinced that their most important buyer persona was a contractor performing commercial construction, even though the data told us that do-it-yourself weekend warriors were a huge potential market for their tools.

Because of their misconception, they wanted us to write content about the products that men in construction might relate to, e.g., pieces on selecting the right chain or blade for a piece of equipment or how much horsepower a given machine might feature. Our research showed that it was women, not men, who were performing the searches that led to sales, and they were looking into projects they'd like complete on their homes, not searching for the tools to do them.

It's no secret that women flock to Pinterest when brainstorming such endeavors, and two months after we convinced the powers that be to deploy a strategy there, a quarter of their total website traffic was originating from the social project planning website. And it just kept growing: the more we put on Pinterest, the more traffic increased to the website, and the longer each visitor remained on the site. Before long, some of our content had been shared over three thousand times and generated over twenty thousand hits a month. Although the leads that were coming in were male names, they had been submitted almost exclusively by female visitors.

Of course, any company can fall victim to misjudging their customer base. We once worked with a sunglass manufacturer whose amazing product was born when the mountain biking CEO became frustrated by the low quality of other options on the market. Although these sunglasses are useful to almost anyone engaged in an active, outdoor lifestyle, until recently, their marketing had been directed almost entirely at the group they were originally designed for—mountain bikers.

The trouble with this strategy is twofold: it requires competing for revenue with companies offering a more diverse range of biking-related products, and it ignores the potential for sales in any number of other underserved, low barriers to entry markets. We took a different course, testing close to two hundred Facebook ads with an assortment of imagery, calls to action, and product benefits to find out what aspects of the sunglasses people valued most.

As you might expect, the ultimate goal was to capture email addresses and find out what groups of people were most interested in this particular pair of shades. The results were surprising to the company: its leads weren't just limited to mountain bikers, but included fishermen, hunters, ice climbers, police officers, and firemen, most of whom owned more expensive high-end sunglasses and were hungry for a cheaper alternative that offered the same quality.

The only reason we discovered that information is because we were able to divorce the company from its preconceived notions about its customer base and test for growth-driven data. Once we had that data, we were able to create buyer personas that zeroed in on people who were already interested in the company's product and who were much more eager to buy.

It should be clear by now that the creation of buyer personas plays a critical role in our process, but there are many misconceptions about them. At one end of the spectrum, there are companies so focused on deliverables that they rush through the persona creation process and end up with an incomplete picture of their ideal client. At the other end are those who romanticize their personas and spend weeks crafting a novel on the intimate relationships of their potential customers.

Both groups are missing the point, which is to identify the different needs the prospects in question have in a way that helps uncover opportunities that competitors who don't understand their customers might miss.

Consider the field of IT security, where one of our clients partners with IBM and deals primarily with companies' chief information security officers. It would be easy to assume that the people working in that field are all Star Wars nerds and churn out fifty articles about how Star Wars and IT security work together—we actually did produce one piece imagining how differently the movies might have gone if the Empire had a better handle on its data. But a buyer persona has to analyze people on a deeper level, determining who they are and what they want, where they're looking to grow, and what's going to solve the problems that keep them up at night.

At the same time, marketers can't just write product material all day long, because even the most dedicated IT security professionals are going to get bored with that after a while. Instead, one of the first things our process requires is an analysis of the kind of publications the people in a given field read, what information they look for on a regular basis, and what kind of websites they might want to visit. Then we ask how and why they are seeking that material, and we ask those questions in a very purposeful way, because the process is ultimately about forming a dialogue that reveals meaningful insights into who they are—both as professionals and as human beings.

Those details will become increasingly valuable as prospects become leads and begin to move through a company's sales funnel. They can help inform marketers' decisions regarding content, aid salespeople in connecting with their leads on a personal level and help foster an environment where customers feel like the organization which with they're partnering "gets them."

The importance of those factors cannot be overstated, but there's another reason buyer personas are so fundamental to successful growth-driven decision making: they don't cost anything. Sure, it takes a little time and effort to put them together, but the capital outlay they require is minimal compared to the impact they can have on a company's bottom line.

It's certainly a cheaper solution than attempting to compete on AdWords, where industry giants such as Cisco and Oracle are pouring tons of money into standard marketing approaches. A smaller company is never going to be able to spend $8,000 per lead, and some of the AdWords in that particular industry go for upward of $200 per click. That's why we consider buyer personas the secret sauce of our method, because they allow us to produce equal or better results for a fraction of the cost.

Perhaps more importantly, using buyer personas allows us to custom-tailor our approach to the people most likely to want what we're selling. When we did a paid test on Facebook for the sunglasses company mentioned earlier, we discovered that people between thirty-three and forty-seven were a prime demographic for their product, so we immediately went to work on a piece called "40 Things Every Guy Should Do Before Turning 40."

By playing on feelings of nostalgia and the inherent desire men have to do some cool things before they reach middle age, we were able to attract the type of people to whom we could sell these particular sunglasses. The key to our success was simple. We looked beyond the niche market the company thought it had and discovered a plethora of other activities their customers loved to do and for which their product was the perfect accoutrement.

We couldn't have discovered this without our buyer personas, the importance of which should be well established by now. But what kind of questions yield the type of information we're looking for? How do we go about unlocking the aspects of our customers' personalities that will help us connect with them in a meaningful way? Consider these opening gambits:

1. What title best describes them?
2. What is their demographic information?
3. What is their job and level of seniority?
4. What does a day in their life look like?
5. What are their pain points? What do you help them solve?
6. What do they value most? What are their goals?
7. Where do they go for information?
8. What experience are they looking for when seeking out your products or services?
9. What are their most common objections to your product or service?

These questions should be enough to set any decent marketer on the path to creating a fleshed-out buyer persona, but it's important to remember that even the best set of questions in the world won't help if they're asked in the wrong setting. We've discovered that a one-hour persona meeting with individual key members of the company conducted face-to-face is the ideal way to extract this information. This is true for a number of reasons, but the biggest ones are that meeting in person allows you to observe the subject's body language while having the discussion, and keeping it brief prevents you from crossing over into the kind of overly detailed territory that's unlikely to be beneficial.

Even though we want the initial meeting to be brief, the truth is you will never be entirely done with buyer personas: you need to revisit them each quarter to ensure that you aren't leaving out key new information, or that changes to the product itself haven't affected the way it's perceived by the target audience. In reality, that concept extends well beyond the realm of buyer personas and ties into the very heart of both inbound marketing and growth-driven decision making. All three rely on a culture that communicates continual revision rooted in close attention to what data proves is best.

It won't always be easy, but when difficulties arise, you can draw attention back to the SMART goal your company is pushing toward as a means of refocusing support. Done properly, this helps reinforce the idea that if something produces results, it continues to be done, and if it doesn't, it gets cut. Outperformers must always win regardless of whose idea they are advancing, and a constant commitment to change that produces results has to be observed at all times.

Without those points of focus, companies often give in to the notion that a person's ideas define their work, thus incentivizing that individual to continue pushing the idea in question regardless of whether it yields results or not. It makes sense: people want to be given praise. If you break down those walls and constantly foster a commitment to results, that same employee is suddenly free to have both great ideas and terrible ones without the latter threatening his or her sense of purpose.

Assuming that this culture is in place, you should be able to reach an agreement on a given buyer persona by the end of the hour-long meeting. Then you can move on to the fun part, which is to create a plan based around your newfound knowledge.

CHAPTER 3

MARKETING TO THE BUYER PERSONA

With a well-defined goal in mind and a clear idea of the kind of customers needed to achieve it, a company implementing the Hüify method for growth-driven decision making is finally primed to begin its marketing efforts in earnest. It's through this process that the company will not only attract the leads it needs to turn into customers but also cultivate the information salespeople need to do just that.

Now the question becomes: where should you begin with your marketing?

One of the first hurdles companies often encounter during their initial forays into writing blog posts is figuring out where to start. As a marketer, you may have received approval to move forward and generated a ton of ideas, but there's a very real possibility of becoming crippled by the blank page in front of you and resorting to writing content that no one cares about outside of the people sharing the room with you.

Company culture manifestos might bring in an applicant or two, but they don't drive revenue. What will drive revenue are content pieces that answer questions your future and existing customers are asking. By focusing on existing customers first, you can often show value from the very beginning simply by keeping them happy. Your work may even result in a salesperson being able to upsell existing customers or renew their contract—something that goes a long way toward building the kind of trust with a company's leadership that's so vital to a successful strategy.

How do you know what questions to answer? Start by asking the people on the front lines: customer service and sales representatives. As the public face of your company, these often undervalued customer service representatives likely have a clearer picture of the issues your customers are facing than even the most educated marketer does. Pick their brains, and you'll discover they're not only eager to share but likely have some thoughts on how to improve the customer experience in general.

Once you have a list of their top-fifty frequently asked questions, sort them by level of potential impact, then create articles that address customers' questions and generate traffic. Not only have you kick-started the content creation process by using this method, but you've also given your marketing strategy instant value in the eyes of the company's leadership, whose concerns will likely be less focused on the content itself than with meeting their budget.

By creating results from the start, you're preemptively answering the questions every CEO, CFO, and COO will inevitably ask of their marketers: Why are you earning the salary you're earning? Why are we investing in the marketing tools you're using every month? How do all of these things tie together with the bottom-line revenue?

With those concerns safely put to bed, marketers can provide themselves the cushion from criticism that is necessary to move into more esoteric inbound efforts without having the process questioned every step of the way. It's in those efforts that the Hüify method demands a different application of the inbound strategy than most marketers are currently offering.

To one degree or another, everyone practicing inbound marketing is operating on essentially the same playbook:

provide content relevant to problems potential customers are facing and let them move themselves toward purchasing your product organically. Admittedly, the simplicity of this method is part of its beauty. It holds people accountable for completing minimum requirements, and if they stick to that framework, they will see results.

Remember, many of the companies implementing inbound are making the initial transition from an outdated traditional form of marketing (TV or radio commercials, for example) to their first taste of Internet marketing. It would be almost impossible for them to not see some degree of success, so it becomes difficult to see how traditional strategies might be improved or made more efficient.

That said, applying the same recipe over and over again has a tendency to lull people into a sense of complacency, and because many marketing agencies would rather compete on price as opposed to value, there's a strong incentive to do the minimum amount of work that will provide results to a client. Because that attitude is so pervasive—and because many clients are relying on these so-called experts to tell them what they need—there's been a proliferation of generalized plans that aren't custom-tailored to the businesses they're supposed to be serving.

A perfect example of this would be a proposal that focused

exclusively on deliverables, offering a monthly package of four blog posts per month, an ebook, a landing page, and an occasional email campaign for, let's say, $3,000 per month. Sure, that will show some traction, but an experienced marketer will immediately see several flaws in the plan.

When kicking off a content marketing plan, you may not see any significant amount of traffic to your content until months after it has been written. Let me explain. You and I become organic traffic for a website when we search for something on Google for and we click on one of the search results. If we are like 67.6% of people then we will click one of the top 5 results.[1] It will take Google about 3 months to rank a new piece of content,[2] so even though you have some killer, interesting, valuable content—it won't be clicked on by 67.6% of people for 3 months and that is if it ranks in the top 5 results.

What was that you say? What if it doesn't rank in the top 5 results? Well then it won't get as many organic search result clicks by a significant margin. This is why it is so important to create more content up front, and get it published as quickly as possible. In 3 months you want to have a bunch of content to be able to test and rank within the top 5 spots.

1 https://moz.com/blog/google-organic-click-through-rates-in-2014
2 http://www.websitemuscle.com/how-long-does-it-take-to-rank-on-google/

This kind of thinking forms the overarching theme of the Hüify method, which is centered on leading our clients toward adopting a goal-focused mindset that favors process over personalities and iteration over specific ideas. A central aspect to the success of that philosophy advocates an approach to website design and marketing similar in style to agile software development—one where the design, code, analysis, and testing of a given project are conducted in unison and often simultaneously in an effort to constantly refine the ultimate product.

Why isn't everyone doing this? I would argue that part of it stems from a lack of understanding of how to track and measure deliverables—and make no mistake, deliverables are hard to produce. Assuming you're not working with an agency, it takes a lot of time to write an article, especially if you aren't a writer and are fairly new to the marketing position you're in. Doing the minimum amount of work in that situation is probably exhausting, so it makes sense that people in those circumstances might feel pretty good about what they're putting out. Since there likely aren't good metrics in place, there's no way to accurately measure their success anyway.

Suppose that isn't the case, and the people involved want to create truly unique content that will produce results. How would they go about it?

For the sake of this example, let's borrow from the IT professionals whose buyer personas we discussed in the previous chapter. Despite our warnings about assuming all such workers are Star Wars fanatics, let's assume we learned they really do love Star Wars to a stereotypical extreme.

That being the case, we can begin to plan content around dates and events that we know they're likely to find significant. May 4th of each year is universally recognized as an unofficial holiday celebrating the films ("May the 4th be with you"), so we'd likely plan a special series of blog posts in the lead-up to the holiday, or, at the very least, something significant for the day itself. With additional films coming out that will add to the story, we know it's important to be prepared with content themed around their impending arrival.

However, it can even go deeper than that. A typical group might ask what conferences their target audience is likely to attend, but because we have a more complex understanding of our customers, we might try to determine what attractions they would be interested in that share locations with the conferences in question. If we learned that large portions of the IT industry are food lovers, we can produce content about the top restaurants in the city they'll be visiting. Similarly, if we discovered that they have an unlikely love for electronic dance music, we can do a little research and serve up locations of the best clubs.

It's not hard to connect the dots and see that generating traffic goes hand in hand with being interested in your customers as human beings. Make no mistake, people appreciate when companies know them and take the time to make that connection, whether it's with humor or commonalities.

With that said, having a terrific buyer persona to work around is not without its own potential downfalls, which primarily manifest themselves in the temptation to produce fun content all day, every day. The IT professionals you want to do business with may love Star Wars, and you may love it, too, but in reality, writing about that and that alone is not going to sell any more software. You may get a ton of visitors from such posts, but they're likely to simply read the pieces and then move on to the next thing without becoming a lead or even considering a purchase. It's all right to do that once or twice, but any more than that and you're writing to educate, not to convert.

This misconception can cause people to go well beyond "fluff" pieces like the Star Wars series we've used as an example and cross into truly educational territory that does little for a company's revenue stream. Sometimes, it leads people to write deep, thoughtful solutions to meaningful problems so well constructed that the reader doesn't need to take any action afterward. By contrast, if the writer shared three quarters of that information and requested an email address to view the rest, they could use the same concept to capture leads and ultimately close them in a sale.

However, it's not just a matter of gaining their business. The reality is that these prospects probably have five or six other problems you could help them with, but the only way you can uncover those is by getting them on the phone. Your product or service might solve all of their issues, but if you allow the visitor to bounce of the page without giving them an opportunity to convert, you can't help them or yourself. There has to be a call to action—something that provides an incentive for prospects to turn themselves into leads—and you have to evaluate just how much information you're willing to give away for free. In practice, that call to action at the end of a piece might look something like this:

"Inbound marketing is definitely here to stay. The best part about it is that it puts more money in your pocket and churns out satisfied customers too. With the above information, you're now on your way to using this strategy to increase profits. What is inbound marketing? How do I use the inbound marketing methodology for my business? Click here to find out."

Even after you've gotten a handle on the difference between writing to educate and writing to convert, it will still be tempting to assume that your product or service will sell itself. As we've already discussed, people don't research products, they research problems, and following this path precludes the possibility that you might be able to customize your product to the customer's needs.

One out of every one hundred potential prospects may determine that the concepts discussed in your article relate to their problem, but if you had conversations with all one hundred of them, you might have been able to talk 20 percent through to this same conclusion. The fact is most articles are going to be written in a generic manner because they need to attract multiple diverse audiences. Even among your narrowed down personas, there's still a great deal of differing priorities amongst these groups. Individual people have unique problems specific to their business and may not be able to decipher their own custom-tailored solution from a blog post meant for mass appeal. Even if you write a piece that a single audience can identify with exactly, it's still going to be read by others who may have reservations that you could address if you had a conversation with them. Instead of leaving the majority of people hanging at the end of your post—expecting them to be so enchanted with your content that they find themselves calling you up to place an order that second—tell them what the next step is. Call them to action.

It helps to think of things in terms of content sharing. It would be easy to assume that if the content of a given article is good enough, it will be shared regardless of whether there are social media buttons located on the page with it or not. For some readers, this may well be true, but what about those who aren't technologically savvy enough to copy and paste the link into Facebook and distribute it to their friends? What if the reader isn't even thinking about sharing because he or she is too busy trying to solve a problem?

No matter the situation, putting those buttons on the page keeps content sharing at the top of readers' minds and makes it more likely that they will act. If you take an extra step and actually ask them to share it, you'll have even better results because it will remind them that doing so provides value to their friends and colleagues. Some may resist this philosophy because they perceive it as being pushy or begging for shares, but the results speak for themselves, and, above all else, results are what should be driving any marketer's decisions.

The same growth-driven, data-centered concepts can be applied to a company's approach to search engine optimization (SEO), something that's often viewed as a mystical unicorn no one can describe but that everyone wants to capture. In reality, it's pretty simple: SEO is the process of making sure search engines know that a certain website has the right answers to whatever question a person is asking. By that measure, simply publishing web pages that provide answers is SEO. Some experts will disagree, claiming that there are algorithms that can be gamed to increase rankings, but if you're starting from the ground level, you don't need to play games to attract visitors. That can be done by writing for the person first and the search engine second.

Traffic is the currency of the web, and certainly the currency of search engines, so there's a temptation for many marketers to engage in deceptive behavior, such as putting a bunch of keywords in white text on a white background or embedding them in code in order to get ahead. Eventually, actual people are going to look at a site, and when they do, they're going to immediately leave because the content likely has nothing to do with what they want. The content does not solve their problem or answer the question they have.

We chose a different method, which begins by writing an

entire article in plain, human English that solves a problem our visitor might have. Then we'll review the article and look for logical, genuine opportunities to add keywords that contribute depth. We won't say we're promoting "the best cafe in Wilmington, North Carolina, on the East Coast," but we might call it the "best health food cafe" instead of simply the "best cafe." It's a tweak that might make the piece wordier, but ultimately doesn't change the meaning and perhaps can even add value by linking to this hypothetical cafe's healthy menu.

The point is, if you continually focus on value, you're going to do pretty well at SEO without becoming an expert at it. Remember, a search engine wants to show the most relevant information first, and as we've already mentioned, that isn't on your homepage, which only contains a fraction of the available information on what your company does and how valuable it is.

In the words of Neil Patel (@neilpatel), "SEO copywriting is all about creating useful, compelling, and valuable content, which targets specific keywords so that other people will gladly promote it on social media platforms. This increases the authority and relevance of your content and improves its ranking in Google for the selected keywords." Neil gives a great example of what SEO-optimized titles would look like for fitness-centered content.

Consider his examples:

- *10 Workout Secrets For Women That Work*
- *Best Ways To Lose 10 Pounds After Pregnancy*
- *Personal Trainer Kits: Become A Certified Personal Trainer*

The following is an example of titles written for search engines. These titles may rank well, but what good is ranking if no one wants to click on your spammy headlines? This is what not to do:

- *Workout Secrets Tips Tricks Lose Weight Fast*
- *Lose 10 Pounds Weight Loss Baby Weight After Pregnancy*
- *Become Certified Personal Trainer Free Certification*

SEO-optimized headlines such as Neil's examples above are the topic of some debate, with many arguing that they represent a disingenuous "clickbait" that reduces the value of content on the web. As a result of that stereotype, many companies avoid writing in this style altogether. However, the truth is, unless you're crying wolf with absurd headlines (*Twitter Shuts Down and Fires All Employees*, for example), it's highly unlikely that headlines of this ilk will cause people to doubt the veracity of the content you're providing.

What it will do is get them to click the link in the first place, which is the primary goal of headline writing. In reality, this delicate balance between subtle keyword manipulation and the importance of providing quality content is necessary to generate traffic and extends well beyond the realm of headline writing and into the copy itself.

Consider the following examples from a post advising business owners on how to enhance their presence on Facebook.

UNOPTIMIZED

Getting onto Facebook is typically the first move made in the social media marketing initiative for new or old businesses alike. It has reached a point where being on social media is an expectation, and you run the risk of seeming out of touch if you aren't. So naturally we have a situation where many businesses are unaware of what to do with their page (and other social media pages). Instead of opting for a "social media intern" by default, take a stab at learning the platform first. No, it isn't rocket science, but there are many pitfalls, poor practices, and misconceptions that are important to know (so you can avoid them). On the flipside, there are opportunities that can greatly help your business and your efforts.

OPTIMIZED

Getting onto Facebook for your business is typically the first move made in the social media marketing initiative for new or old businesses alike. It has reached a point where having Facebook for business is an expectation, and you run the risk of seeming out of touch if you don't have a Facebook for your business. So, naturally we have a situation where many businesses are unaware of what to do with their Facebook business page (and other social media pages). Instead of opting for a "social media intern" by default, take a stab at learning the Facebook business platform first. No, it isn't rocket science, but there are many pitfalls, poor practices, and misconceptions that are important to know (so you can avoid them). On the flipside, there are great opportunities that can greatly help your business and your efforts using Facebook for business.

It may seem simple, but there are two ways this can go wrong, and both are equally worrisome. A digital marketer might dive straight into the available data and end up giving in to the temptation to try and cram as many keywords as possible into every page (see the "Optimized" example above). At the opposite end of the spectrum, someone who comes from a writing background might be more inclined to produce tons of helpful content without any thought toward SEO (the "Unoptimized" example).

In one case, the copy sounds like a robot who's overly focused on keywords wrote the piece, which ultimately portrays the company itself in a negative light. In the other, the copy never gets seen because it lacks the necessary qualities to connect with the people looking for it.

The following are four of the biggest mistakes companies make when producing content, including the keyword mistake we just reviewed.

- Ignoring the Analytics: This is the worst pitfall. Metrics are key to the success of your content strategy. Which topics get the most views? Which titles get the most clicks on social? What time of day are most people reading your blog? Where are they sharing it? The answers to these questions will help you refine your content and better attract your potential customers.
- Self-Promotion: Imagine having a conversation with someone who only talked about him or herself. As anyone who's ever been on a miserable blind date can attest, you wouldn't want to stay in that conversation very long. It's very common for a company to want write about itself—a new location, awards it may have won—because it's a topic it cares about deeply and has a lot of knowledge on. Sadly, your customer doesn't care, and you come off braggy.

- Keyword Stuffing: Not fully understanding keyword techniques can be very harmful. It's as if many of today's marketing professionals think, "Keywords help me rank on Google? Great, I'll just cram my posts full of them!" No. Google's main priority is user experience, and it will go out of its way to guard readers from scary content. Keywords are one component of SEO, and while bearing a large impact in the grand scheme, they can have a severely negative impact if abused.
- Personal Opinion: Writing inbound copy is a creative endeavor, and as with all such matters, there can be a temptation to allow one's personal preferences to interfere with what might be best from a professional perspective. "I don't like that topic so I'm not going to write about it," some marketers think and understandably so. Stepping outside of personal opinions and beliefs about an industry can be hard for business owners. A company's deep investment in its brand can often narrow its scope and prevent it from fully catering to what its customers want.

Suppose you avoid those dangerous temptations and succeed at writing effective copy that converts visitors into leads. What other eventualities might a savvy marketer need to be watching for? One of the main things to keep in mind is that the online ecosystem changes constantly:

apps are being developed right now that will dominate their markets and lead traffic—and even revenue—in a few short years.

By contrast, human beings tend to gravitate toward the way things have always been done, and when they do decide to change, they'll often research the potential change until they're blue in the face, allowing months to pass before they do something as basic as launching a new website. Avoiding these pitfalls is of paramount importance because every month spent evaluating things in a vacuum is a month spent without results that could dictate more effective revisions. The lost opportunity cost is huge because the traction you could have had ends up being squandered.

Yes, the website needs to be user friendly, and it can't be riddled with typos, but as long as it communicates what needs to be communicated, you're better off having something that's done rather than something that's perfect. A finished live product can be tested, measured, and improved upon—all things that can't happen during development—and the results can be huge.

That kind of success hinges on a culture of iteration, which doesn't come naturally to many companies because there is a very real fear of failure. It is understood that a significant increase in the number of tests run equates to a significant amount of failure—not a personal failure or even a company failure, but the failure of an individual test.

Imagine putting up two ads, one of which is blue and the other is red. Perhaps the blue ad performed poorly because it was used on Facebook where a big portion of the site itself is blue and thus likely to wash out anything with a similar hue. Now imagine you're the person in the group whose idea fueled the production of the blue ad.

You may believe that the failure of that ad speaks directly to your ability to do your job, but with an interactive culture in place, nothing could be further from the truth. Instead of viewing your work in a negative light, everyone on the team shares in the responsibility for it and benefits from the opportunity to learn something from its failure. Why? Because they have a cultural commitment to what works and no one is wed to their individual ideas.

Of course, adopting this mindset is not without challenges: companies often have a hard time allocating resources to testing because they don't think it equals productivity or growth, amounting to little more than research. A quick comparison of this method with more traditional means of marketing reveals that the necessary investment actually pales in comparison to what a company might already be doing.

Consider the results of a direct-mail campaign, the most highly effective iterations of which convert about 2 percent of the targeted leads into customers. The implication of this statistic is that infuriating 98 percent of one's potential customers with unwanted marketing material is considered success. It seems crazy, but some companies continue to allocate millions of dollars to these ridiculously inefficient endeavors.

And it's not as if in-person marketing is any more cost effective. Booth space at the average industry conference is likely to cost upward of $40,000, making it extremely unlikely that the cost per lead generated by being there will produce a worthwhile return—if one occurs at all. After all, you have no control over the environment in which your booth is located, and whatever materials you're presenting could easily be upstaged by a more flashy distraction in the immediate area. Depending on just how flashy it is, it might render your entire investment futile.

It's true that testing the best means of converting a large number of leads isn't free, but one advantage is that, even while doing so, you're still getting leads. By its very nature, growth-driven decision making requires a company to grow even while testing, which is sometimes difficult for those unfamiliar with the concept to wrap their heads around.

Even if that wasn't the case, testing is still a better investment of resources because the end product—be it blog posts or a better website in general—will continue to exist and potentially attract leads long after the initial expenditure. Even alternate forms of web-based advertising can't make that claim, as pay-per-click campaigns and their ilk all eventually come to a conclusion, whereas websites and blog posts remain the company's perpetual property.

That distinction makes testing a series of blog articles more like an investment than an expense: a relatively inexpensive initial move can very easily yield compounding returns for years to come. Unlike print, television, or in-person advertising, an additional advantage blog posts is that those articles will always appear in an environment the company controls.

These ideas are so logical, the only resistance they typically receive stems from pride and insecurity, a point that's been driven home for me lately as I've worked to nurture a relationship with a North Carolina airport. The executives in charge of their marketing campaign have been investing $15,000 per month in radio and TV advertising despite the fact that neither have seen or heard the ads themselves in months. Why not? They don't listen to radio or watch traditional television. They admitted they listen to Spotify and watch Netflix. To this we responded: "So do your customers."

Cue the mic drop.

It should be clear to any rational person that the status quo isn't working, but there's still a resistance to trying something new. If it works, they've just been proven wrong, and if it doesn't, they're afraid they may go from operating at 20 percent efficiency to 5 percent or worse. To break through these barriers and create a culture that will generate results, it's imperative that we bring the focus back to our goal. None of us knows what the future holds, and although we can make reasonable guesses, it's impossible to predict how every person will respond to every situation.

With that in mind, the best way to protect any organization is to try a multitude of approaches to see how they perform.

This strategy not only aids in the alignment of sales and marketing, but it can also unify an entire company, inspiring the people involved to make sure the product is ready to scale and the staff is ready to support new customers.

The only question that remains is: how do we convert these leads, generated by the marketing efforts we've discussed so far, into customers?

CHAPTER 4

HANDING OFF TO SALES

There's no doubt that employing the growth-driven mentality we've discussed so far will result in an extremely effective marketing campaign that will convert vast numbers of website visitors into sales leads. That's been proven time and time again by our experiences creating and refining our method. But what happens next? Will those leads be so blown away by the combination of your company's blog posts and products that they'll close themselves?

The suggestion may sound ridiculous, but believe it or not, many marketers are operating under that misconception. They think simply beginning the process is enough—that their product or service is so good, people will buy immediately if they are only presented with the opportunity.

This line of thinking is especially prominent among companies operating in the tech space, where there exists a near-universal dedication to the idea that salespeople can close leads by simply scheduling a demonstration, conducting that demonstration, and making a proposal. On the surface that may seem like a reasonable process, but it's important to remember that you're dealing with smart, well-informed buyers who understand both why the product might be beneficial and why it might be detrimental.

Perhaps they see potential problems that your website didn't do a good enough job refuting—problems that might cause more work for them, require more management, or even necessitate the addition of entirely new tasks they wouldn't have had they not purchased your product. Perhaps they think the product is too complex for the technical skills of the team they're representing. Or, perhaps the demonstration focuses on the wrong aspects of the product—those built to address problems the lead doesn't have rather than the ones suited to the company's unique issue(s).

In each of these cases and dozens of others, it's highly unlikely that even a truly adept salesperson can close a lead on the strength of the demonstration alone. There are simply too many variables that can't be accounted for—unless, of course, someone were to have an actual conversation with the prospect beforehand and determine the specific issues that caused him or her to become a lead in the first place.

To see why this is so important, put yourself in the shoes of a hypothetical buyer looking for a way to speed up your company's quote creation process. Imagine that the existing system requires salespeople to request a quote from the organization's accounting department—which a third party must approve—before they can forward that information to potential clients. Having determined that the process is unduly burdensome, you've turned to the web in search of software that will facilitate salesperson access to these processes and, ideally, increase the speed and efficiency with which they can close leads.

Now imagine you've discovered software with three primary functions: reporting, automation, and the access system that drove you to search for it in the first place. Although the two other features may well prove useful, you are principally concerned with the third because it's what addresses the issue most important to you. Which do you think you're most likely to be interested in when it comes time to seeing a demonstration?

If the someone from the company conducting the demonstration hasn't taken the time to find out the answer to that question, you're going to get the standard-issue presentation, even though 80 percent of it may focus on the two features you couldn't care less about. By the time the presenter gets around to discussing the thing you came to see, you would have tuned out completely.

It goes without saying that this system needs work, and the best marketing campaign in the world won't save a sale if this is what the prospect is faced with after finally getting on a demo. As any sportsman can tell you, once you've hooked a fish, you still have to reel it in, and inbound marketing is little more than highly effective bait.

To see real results, an organization needs to carry the philosophy's communicative principles—the recognition that people are searching for answers to problems companies are capable of solving and both parties can find those solutions cooperatively—directly into its sales process.

Not only will this result in a more effective sales process, it will shift the salesperson into the frame of a consultant, allowing him or her to challenge the lead's thinking and perhaps identify underlying issues of which the would-be customer isn't even aware. Repeated viewings of *Glengarry Glen Ross* may have salespeople thinking they should "always be closing," but in the era of the Internet, "always be helping" is a far more effective paradigm. By accepting it, salespeople put themselves in a position to add value to the product as opposed to relying on the customer to infer how valuable it might be from a presentation or the marketing material they've seen.

Those are things even the best inbound strategy can't achieve. When executed perfectly, marketing is only going to take the buyer a quarter of the way down the sales funnel (a visual representation of a company's sales process at scale). There are multiple other steps a customer must take before reaching the end of that funnel, and at each turn, there are dozens of opportunities—just like the one discussed earlier—for them to lose interest or decide not to buy.

Just how bad are the odds that a lead will turn into a closed sale? As a hypothetical example, let's say ten thousand people per month see some piece of a company's marketing material. For this example, let's say that piece of marketing material is a website.

Statistically, an average of 1 percent of this group of ten thousand will submit an email address or some other piece of information the company can use to follow up. That means out of that initial group of ten thousand, we now have one hundred leads in various degrees of qualification ranging from those who want to do business now to those who just wanted whatever free piece of information they were offered in order to facilitate the collection of their contact details.

If you've paid attention so far, you know that the next step is for that company's salespeople to call these leads and qualify them. For the sake of this example, let's say ten are ready to move forward in some form or fashion. In our experience, about 20 percent of that group of ten will go on to eventually do business with you, which means that after all that effort, you now have two customers.

Does this sound rather uninspiring? Don't let it worry you too much. Sales funnels vary wildly based on the intricacies of the companies involved, and depending on the industry, those two customers could be worth several hundred thousand dollars in revenue. Regardless of those factors, the steps to capitalize on this information remain the same: an organization can now compare its average monthly sales funnel against its revenue goals and determine how many months it will take to acquire the number of customers it needs or wants.

Using our example, if the goal was to gain twenty new customers, we now know it would take about ten months to do so. Having gathered all this information, we can begin the process of analyzing it and improving the results.

The easiest way to do this is to ask questions. Why is there only a 1 percent conversion rate on the website? How can we get the website to convert higher? Why are we only qualifying 10 percent of our leads? If they're becoming a lead, shouldn't they be a little more interested in what we're selling? Does that mean our messaging is off? Why are they filling out forms but not interested in the product we're selling? Why are we only closing 20 percent of the people who are qualified? If they're qualified, that means that they can buy our product and that they're interested in buying it, so why aren't we closing more of them?

To determine the answer to most, if not all, of these questions we must examine the company's sales process instead of dissecting its marketing efforts. More than any other factor, we've found that lengthy response times are the cause of a great number of woes experienced by companies struggling to convert more leads.

That's one of the primary reasons we've come to favor immediate, instant follow-up, preferably within five minutes of receiving a new lead. From a logistical standpoint, having such quick response times increases the odds that a salesperson will get in touch with a human being rather than leaving a message on a machine that will almost certainly be ignored. When they do talk to that real, live person, it will be during a time when the problem the lead is trying to solve is at the forefront of his or her mind.

Not only does this instant follow-up make the lead more receptive to an appropriately helpful caller, it also makes him or her more likely to ultimately become a customer. Research has shown that as many as 50 percent[3] of customers buy from the first person who calls them, and calling within five minutes virtually guarantees that person will be you.

How much of a difference does being first really make? When we committed to making the change in our own sales process, we reduced the length of Hüify's sales cycle from nine months to three weeks—all because we began contacting people while their problem was still fresh on their minds.

Remember, the cooperative approach to sales and marketing advocated by the inbound philosophy differs from other forms of marketing in that it seeks to solve problems customers already know they have (as opposed to telling them they have a problem they didn't know about and then offering a solution). Marketing materials, sales calls, and every other step along the path to closing a deal are all designed to be as helpful to customers as possible, so

3 "Research shows that 35-50% of sales go to the vendor that responds first." -InsideSales.com

why not offer them those resources when they're already looking for them?

There's no logical reason not to, yet companies continue to ignore this seemingly obvious wisdom, and they miss out on a huge source of opportunity as a result. Even organizations with truly impressive, highly regarded products fall victim to this kind of thinking, often because they lack the technological infrastructure necessary to facilitate a truly instant response to new leads.

Although there are several ways of creating such a system, we've found it's best achieved with the use of customer relationship management (CRM) software that notifies salespeople the moment a new lead is generated, allowing them to act on the information in an ultra-timely fashion. We witnessed the profound effects of implementing this kind of software firsthand while working with a virtual CFO firm whose product is so buttoned up, companies often hire them to investigate and cleanup cases of fraud or to perform due diligence ahead of a major merger or acquisition.

All of their customers are ecstatic and their retention rates are insane, but until recently they've had almost no online presence at all. In fact, even though they've been in business for close to a decade, 90 percent of their customers were coming from referrals alone. Predictably, that all changed the second we launched their new website and began analyzing the type of questions they are frequently asked during sales calls.

Once we crafted a series of articles addressing those issues, their traffic exploded. It wasn't long before their number of leads followed suit, and since they were primarily composed of people looking to solve accounting problems, it's not hard to imagine the urgency with which these potential customers wanted their issues addressed.

An influx of new leads that overwhelming in scope meant the company needed an infrastructure that facilitated acting on those leads quickly—a uniquely challenging proposition for this particular organization since its CEO had historically handled every sales conversation. That was easy to do when leads were coming in at a slow, steady clip, but the dramatic increase brought about by our efforts on the web meant the team would need to become flexible enough to dip out of meetings, and in some cases, step into leadership roles, whenever the volume of leads made it necessary.

What exactly do those sales conversations look like? What other conversations should happen as a lead moves further down the sales funnel?

Like most other sales processes, ours begins with an initial connect call, which is primarily about establishing a relationship with a lead. Remember, the sooner you make this call the better, because that's when the lead is in the middle of asking questions and trying to figure out what to do to solve a problem. Your goal should be to ask your own questions and provide simple answers to the lead while collecting information on the company's budget, authority, and need and time (BANT), as well as its goal, plan, and challenges (GPC).

A typical connect call lasts about twenty minutes and must result in acquiring this information before you can move to the next step. However, as the name implies, it's also important to establish a connection as well as to challenge the lead's thinking so that the lead exits the call feeling as if he or she spoke with an expert. Here are some examples[4] of how that often plays out for Hüify's sales staff when they are calling on prospects: new leads to past customers. Remember we are helping companies understand that they need to work *with* us for their marketing and sales growth:

INBOUND LEAD REQUESTING A CONSULTATION OR DEMO

(Call immediately, within 5 minutes for optimal results.)

4 Adapted from HubSpot's agency partner sales training

Hi Norman, this is Josh with Hüify. (PAUSE. They will usually be surprised and comment about how fast it was that you called them.) Haha, well I saw that you had some questions and I was in between meetings, so I thought I could help answer them. (PAUSE. Let them start talking).

INBOUND LEAD

Hey, Norman! (PAUSE) It's Josh (PAUSE) from Hüify. (PAUSE. Listen for recognition of your company name here.) Did I catch you at a bad time? I was calling because I saw you downloaded ______ and I wanted to see if it was helpful. Is your company planning to ______? I spent a little time on your website before calling you. Do you mind if I give you a ______ tip?

TARGET ACCOUNT

Hey, Norman! (PAUSE) It's Josh (PAUSE) from Hüify (PAUSE). I saw the blog article that you wrote about ______. I really enjoyed it. (Continue conversation about this commonality.) Can I give you one small suggestion? At the bottom of the article, there isn't a clear next step. Have you thought about what the next logical step would be for the reader if they wanted to follow up with you to ask more questions about this topic?

EXISTING OR FORMER CLIENT

Hi, Norman, how are things going with you? It's been a few months since we ______, and I wanted to see how ______ has been performing. Now that we have the foundation set up, it might make sense to have a discussion about how ______. Do you want to schedule some time to discuss? I can point out some suggestions for ______. When's a good time to chat? I'm available during ______ next week.

MAKE A DECISION

Listen carefully to the prospect's responses, paying close attention to their tone and subtext so that you come to understand their current state of mind. This is an early turning point in the process, and depending on how the conversation unfolds, you'll need to make a decision about what strategy to pursue moving forward.

If the prospect seems open to the conversation taking place:

- Use gentle questioning to gather information about their business
- Based on their answers, share an inbound tip to build trust
- Share a positioning statement
- Based on fit, decide if you should move forward, and book the exploratory call

If the prospect seems to be more reserved:

- Leverage an inbound tip to build trust
- Use a positioning statement to create value
- Listen to determine if your statement and tips are resonating and moving the prospect into a more open frame of mind

If the prospect is in a closed frame of mind, send him or her some free resources (a good blog article or ebook) and politely exit the call.

GATHER BUSINESS INFORMATION

Use the following sample questions as a guide to start gathering relevant business information. Your goal is to determine if the prospect needs help and if you can help. This information will also assist you in preparing you for the exploratory call.

BUSINESS QUESTIONS

- Would it be possible to get a brief overview of your business model?
- How big your your team?
- What kind of person is in your target market? Be as specific as you can.

- What is it that makes your company different than your competitors?
- Why has your company made increasing online visibility a priority?

SALES AND MARKETING QUESTIONS

- How do you currently generate new business?
- What is your existing process for acquiring leads? Is that working well for you?
- How many new leads are you hoping to generate?
- Is there a specific time table for acquiring these leads?
- What is the long term purpose for acquiring these new leads?
- Have you given much thought to the idea of doing something *different* to generate new business?

WEBSITE QUESTIONS

- What's your current process for updating your website?
- Do you currently have a strategy for using blogging and social media?
- Are you currently partnering with any agencies to help with your website or using third party tools?
- If so, how are your relationships with those agencies?

CLOSE THE CALL

"My next suggestion would be to schedule what we call an exploratory call. I can offer some additional tips on [something the lead values] and share what we have seen working for others who are trying to ... [reference goals or pains mentioned during the call]. I'm also interested in hearing more about [goals x, y and z] that you mentioned earlier. Perhaps we can talk a little more about whether there might be a fit between our companies."

WRAP IT UP

"Great, how does [day] at [time] sound?"

Once the call is booked, don't hang up just yet. The moments immediately after booking an exploratory meeting can be a great time to have further conversation and gather additional information. Here is one way to introduce that conversation: "So that I'm a little more prepared for our call next week, would you mind if I asked you a question or two?"

Regardless of what you learn afterward, it's important to wrap up the connect call by scheduling another call and assigning the prospect some homework to complete before moving forward. It doesn't necessarily matter what the homework is, as the goal is to set the stage for the exploratory call by requiring that the lead buy in before it ever begins.

Once you have established that buy-in, it's time to look for deeper insight into both the company as a whole and the individual interests of the people likely to be involved in future calls. Although the primary focus of this exercise is to ensure that you have a plan for whatever direction the conversation may turn, it's also worthwhile to learn the hobbies and interests of the people involved. To accomplish both, peruse a wide variety of available information: the company's website, individuals' social media accounts, and even complementary or competing products.

Most companies are selling a service, which in reality equates to selling time: by hiring your firm, these people expect to gain more of it, and it's not hard to imagine they'll use those extra hours pursuing their interests. Making this connection for them, whether explicitly or implicitly, can sometimes grease the wheels of consideration by shifting focus to the leisure activity gained as opposed to the expense.

With that research under your belt, you will be better prepared for the exploratory call and can focus on its primary purpose: determining the lead's specific goals. If a prospect says he or she need fifty leads by December, for example, you should ask, "Why fifty and not one hundred?" If the prospect says he or she needs to generate $1 million in revenue, the follow-up should be, "Why not $1.1 million? Why not $940,000?" By asking these questions, you can begin to uncover the bigger picture: perhaps if the company generates $1 million, it will have four investors lined up to pour in $1 million each. Suddenly, the engagement just grew from a $1 million venture to a $5 million one, all because you took the time to ask, "Why?"

One way to determine whether an exploratory call has gone well is to measure the total time each person on the call spends speaking. At Hüify, we know that if the salesperson talks more than the prospect, something is wrong, because the goal is to gather as much information about the company as possible. It will be tempting for salespeople to attempt to solve the first problem a prospect puts in front of them, but it's important to remember that there may be several more problems to solve if you can listen long enough to find out about them. Before the call ends, you should make sure everyone's needs are being met and that you have full buy-in from all the major players in the decision. To do that, it's vital that you uncover goals and motivations that are driving the people involved. Perhaps someone's prospects for promotion are based on growing the size of his or her department in addition to revenue, meaning you must now expand your focus to include advertising company culture and the key metrics that will attract new applicants. With those concepts in mind, here are some questions you might ask.

THE COMPANY

- Who are your customers?
- Who are your competitors?
- What makes your company unique?
- What role do you play in your industry?
- What is the average sale price of your [product/service]?
- What is your company's mission?
- Does your company have specific revenue targets?

THE ORGANIZATION (INTRACOMPANY)

- What are the goals of this department?
- What is your role?
- How does your role fit into the company as a whole?
- What are some recent projects you've been working on?
- Are there other roles or duties being performed in your department?
- How does your organization fit into the company as a whole?

BANT

Budget

- What is your current lead generation strategy? (Listen for evidence of and level of marketing investment.)
- Are you making marketing plans for next year? (Listen for evidence of increase or decrease in budget.)
- Has there been a good return on your past marketing investments? (if yes) Do you think you'll increase spending on marketing this year? (if no) Do you think you'll decrease your marketing investment this year? Why or why not?
- What were you planning on investing in marketing to meet your goals? (This is best asked after a thorough goals discussion.)

Authority

- Can you go into a bit more detail about your role in the company?
- What is the typical process for your company to determine whether they want to work with a new partner?

Need

- See "GPC" and "Cost of Inaction" in this section.

Timing

- How much time do you have to make these results happen?
- What's the deadline for achieving [goal]?
- Is there a specific timeline for making [goal] happen?
- In the coming year, what date is most vital to your company? Why?
- What needs to happen in the next two months in order for your timeline to stay on track?
- Is this goal your number one priority right now?
- Are there other priorities on your plate?
- Do you have the infrastructure and resources necessary to implement this plan now?
- Could you benefit from some guidance in determining the specific steps involved in executing this plan so you can figure out the appropriate time to implement each phase?
- If this goal or the timeline to reach it begin to look unrealistic, how likely is it you'll revise them?

GPC

Goals

- What is the one thing that must absolutely be accomplished this year?
- Are there any specific goals your company is

pursuing?

- What are your top-three projects this year/quarter in terms of overall importance?
- Are there published revenue goals for the coming quarter/year?
- What other goals that are important to the company?
- Are there any personal goals that coincide with these company goals?

Plans

- What specific steps are being taken now to achieve [goal]?
- What is your plan to make it happen?
- What is the ultimate goal with the website?
- Did last year's plans for sales or marketing look different than this year's?
- Which parts were successful and which ones did you discard?
- How does that compare to this year in terms of what's changed?
- What does the staffing situation look like in the marketing department?
- In what type of marketing activities are they currently engaged?
- Are there any other activities planned but that haven't been implemented yet?
- Is there a specific campaign designed to support

these strategies?

- What's been most successful?
- Which ones didn't perform so well?
- Where do your best leads originate?
- How many leads does the present strategy generate?
- What is your opinion of that performance?
- Is lead quality at an acceptable level?
- Does your company consider all leads equal?
- Is the sales team conducting cold calls?
- What is the sales team's opinion of the leads?
- If you are cold calling, to whom are these calls being directed?
- Are you buying lists?
- Do those lists prove successful?
- What does the sales department's staffing look like?
- What qualities indicate a lead is "sales ready" to your team?
- How many leads would it take to achieve [goal]?
- Is that target met as often as you'd like?
- What is the cost to acquire new leads/customers?
- Are any efforts being made to reduce your cost per lead?
- What metrics are used to determine the quality of a given strategy?
- What worked last year? What didn't perform so well? Given that information what are you thinking of doing differently this year?

- Do you think xyz might be obstacles to the implementation of your plan?
- Is there an expectation that implementing this plan will go smoothly?
- Are the resources in place to implement this plan?
- Would you like to hear about how other people I've worked with have implemented similar plans?
- Are you open to thinking about reaching these goals in a different manner?

Challenges

- You've given me a terrific picture of what you are hoping to accomplish and what plans are in place to ensure it happens. I'm wondering what obstacles you think might get in your way.
- Are there any known factors that might prevent your plan from working?
- What do you expect to get in the way of achieving [goal]?
- What programs do you already have in place to achieve what we've talked about?
- How is that going?
- That sounds like it might be really hard to do. What are you going to do to ensure that it works?
- What's the biggest challenge facing you from a marketing perspective?
- You've tried to eliminate these problems in the past,

but they seem pretty persistent. What makes you think you'll be able to take care of them this year?

- Is there enough expertise internally to make sure that happens?
- What does the strategy for addressing these challenges look like?
- Suppose it starts to look like this plan isn't going to work and you still have enough time to make adjustments. Will you switch gears?

COST OF INACTION

Some of the following questions address the costs of inaction (consequences), others address the benefits of action (rewards), which is the inverse and can be used in a similar way.

- Is there a belief that doing more of what you're currently doing would be an acceptable way of reaching your goals? Why or why not?
- What happens if you reach your goals? Will it affect you on a personal level?
- What happens if you don't hit the goal? Will it affect you on a personal level?
- Will it matter much if you don't reach your goals?
- Is there a plan for what should take place after hitting the goals?
- Do you get bonuses, stand to get promoted or get

more resources if you can achieve this goal? Will you get fired, lose responsibility, or be demoted if you can't figure this out?

As with the connect call, the exploratory call ends with scheduling another time to speak, but by this point, your focus will have shifted to refuting any possible objections the prospect may have. You can assume that a few additional decision makers have been brought into the loop, so it's important to start by rehashing what was already discussed in the first two calls. Rather than go through the information yourself, a more effective means might be to use an internal advocate—someone you've already spoken to a few times who seems to be on board. You might say, "Gentlemen, thanks so much for meeting with us. We're really excited to talk about some of these possibilities. Jonathan and I have had a couple of great conversation so far, as you probably know. Jonathan, would you mind repeating some of the main facts we covered on why this is an important engagement?"

Instantly, you now have Jonathan, a coworker the other people in the room know and trust, making your pitch for you using language that makes it seem as if the concepts were the company's idea—or maybe even his idea. Remember, Jonathan knows what's going to motivate the other decision makers much better than you do, and it probably won't be long before someone is saying, "Yeah, this is brilliant. This is a great move. Thank you, Jonathan, for pulling all this together. We are really excited to work with you all."

The only remaining caveat is, of course, the budget. Even though you've already discussed it in previous calls, it's human nature to try and get the best deal possible, and we all know this instinct will likely prompt people to keep the amount they're willing to pay close to the vest. A good way to avoid addressing this head-on is to shift focus from the budget itself to the amount and type of work that will need to be done.

Remember when we determined it was important to grow the staff along with the revenue? Using that information, I might say, "One of your main goals is to grow your staffing side by four new employees. Well, as we've discussed, your biggest challenge in this process has been that you've got an amazing culture, you're just not showing it to the rest of the world, so no one really knows how awesome it is to work here. One of the things we're going to need to do is write content that communicates how good your culture is. We've determined that we're going to need to write about ten articles a month that are going to just talk about your culture. What are some of the main concepts that need to be communicated in those articles to get the kind of applicants you're looking for?"

Even though I'm not talking about a budget here, I am asking the customer to grant tacit approval to the amount of work that needs to be done. Once we've agreed on that, I might ask if anyone already employed by the company is currently writing content—and there will almost certainly be someone who is—followed by an inquiry about the other tasks that person is responsible for, what his or her salary is, and how long it takes the person to produce content.

The goal of gathering this information is to determine what they're already paying for the service we'll be providing. Let's say the employee in question makes $50 an hour and requires four hours to complete an article, meaning the company is already spending $2,000 per month for the same content we would be producing for them. Once I point this out and draw attention to the fact that we will be able to do the work for less than that amount, the decision makers and number crunchers become less likely to balk at that particular line item on the proposal we end up sending them.

You can repeat this process for as many line items as necessary before concluding this phase of the call by discussing the contract itself, explaining what it will look like, and describing a range of possible costs within a few thousand dollars of the stated budget. It's important that you don't send them any kind of actual proposal until they've given strong indications that they plan to buy.

To the seasoned salesperson, that advice may seem counterintuitive, but consider what's being subcommunicated when you provide a proposal to someone who hasn't made some sort of purchasing commitment. Rather than viewing your contract as a plan that will solve the lead's problem, you're treating it as little more than free advice and devaluing the time and effort you put into crafting the plan in the first place. It is understood that the odds of closing a lead with that mentality are pretty terrible, and failing to heed this warning is often the cause of a bottleneck at the end of an organization's sales funnel.

Of course, if you've performed the previous steps well, it's very likely that the lead will already have expressed serious interest in doing business with your company. In that case, you can simply tell the organization that you'll have a draft contract sent to them before the fourth—and, hopefully, final—call, so that they can review it for misspelled names, DBAs, or other minutia. The beauty of phrasing things in this manner is that you're asking them to approve the stated price, and in doing so shifting the frame of the conversation to one where purchasing is assumed rather than requested. Altogether, this phase of the conversation should take an hour to an hour and a half, and by its conclusion, you should be ready to make the closing call.

If you've done the previous three calls correctly, this will be the shortest and easiest part of the process. In fact, I've participated in closing calls that took fewer than ten minutes to wrap up. Occasionally, you will encounter resistance, and if that resistance comes in the form of things you've already discussed, that should raise a couple of red flags. One is that it's an indication that the prospect doesn't trust or believe you. The other is that the prospect is likely to challenge you every step of the way, even after he or she agreed to your proposal, making it extremely difficult to do business with the customer over a long term.

Don't make the mistake of expecting the prospect to magically turn into another person the moment he or she signs the contract. You need to address the customer's concerns head-on and, should the situation require it, flat out call the customer out. How can you do that without seeming like a jerk? Simply remind the customer of what he or she already knows: you've discussed everything thoroughly in previous calls, and although you're happy to go over everything with him or her again, that will generate more work for you and your team and thus increase the final price.

One of two things will happen at this point: either the

person objecting will relent—in which case you should close the deal—or you could potentially lose the sale. But even if you lose the sale, it will still be worth it in the long run. You don't want to work with those kinds of people anyway.

Regardless of how this process comes to a close, by this point we've reached the end of our sales funnel. Hopefully, seeing the process play out has inspired a bit of an epiphany: although we often view marketing and sales as disparate entities, the fact is, everything is sales.

Now, I realize sales has become something of a dirty word in today's business climate. People don't want to be associated with the kind of pushy and often uncouth tactics that have come to stereotype the field. By applying the basic principles of inbound marketing (helping interested prospects solve their problems in cooperation with a business partner) to the sales side, we can avoid becoming one of those undesirable caricatures and make the buying process better for everyone involved.

Marketing will become a means of sales support, and the number of conversations necessary to close a deal will dwindle as buyers enter the process in a more educated state. By the time they actually speak to a salesperson, the pushy tactics people want to distance themselves from will be unnecessary because buyers are already primed to purchase organically. After all, why wouldn't they be? You've been providing them with tools that help them solve their problems every step of the way. Buying is the next logical step.

Handling the process of bringing a lead down the sales funnel this way is simple, efficient, and, above all else, effective. But what does it look like when things aren't done properly? Imagine we get a lead in the form of Prospect Steve, who was interested enough in a free ebook we offered on our website to provide his email in exchange for it and was willing to share that he's seeking a way to increase his leads in the process.

Steve receives an initial, automated email and then thirty days later a follow-up email that provides a little more information about our company. Two weeks pass, and maybe because the agency doesn't have as many leads in the pipeline, its salespeople decide to follow up with all of their remaining contacts. Someone calls Prospect Steve, but doesn't connect, so he leaves a voicemail and maybe sends another email. Even though nothing has happened yet, the marketing department at this firm is celebrating because Steve is a lead and a salesperson called him. They think they've done their job and are moving forward.

Of course, nothing could be further from the truth. Steve isn't qualified, his specific needs and goals remain unknown, and the sales staff has allowed ample time for other organizations to make first contact with him. However, because this hypothetical sales staff is operating on the outdated misconceptions this book exists to address, they don't know any of that.

So more time passes, and Steve gets another automated email, which he opens because his need for leads still hasn't been addressed and is now more pressing than ever. He downloads another online resource, prompting the marketing department to inquire as to how far the salespeople have progressed in their efforts to close him. Those salespeople, meanwhile, don't even recognize Steve's name because they were never able to connect, but they call him again at marketing's request.

Unfortunately, too much time has passed. Steve has already gotten busy with something else, so he doesn't answer his phone this time, either. It's not long before the process becomes a self-perpetuating cycle of missed connections and failed efforts to connect. Why? The organization failed to close the deal because the Gap between marketing and sales was too big for the two entities to act in a timely manner, which rendered them unable to help poor Steve, or even themselves.

CHAPTER 5

STICKING TO THE PLAN

The main premise of everything we've discussed so far is that there's a gap between sales and marketing that causes organizations to lose out on significant opportunities. Once they identify it and change it, there's the possibility for exponential growth in a very short period of time because the people involved can finally capitalize on those opportunities that would have otherwise been lost.

Unlike other issues that might necessitate large investments or new staff, closing the Gap requires only that we develop a protocol and a communication system that bridges the Gap and eliminates the barrier between the two departments.

Before we can do all of that, we have to remember why the Gap is there in the first place: the people involved feel the burden is on them to perform at an individual level instead of viewing the company as a team. The primary driver of that attitude is fear, whether it's the fear of getting fired or the fear of missing something that will make them seem ill equipped for their roles. Often, this leads to situations where employees try to take on tasks by themselves when they shouldn't just to prove to the company that they're valuable.

We once worked with a startup where an employee had that exact mentality, despite the fact that the whole team knew she wasn't competent enough to handle the tasks she had been assigned. She contributed very little, but it was a small company and no one wanted to go through the pain of letting her go. In times of transition, she would try to hoard as much information as possible because deep down she knew she wasn't capable of producing results and needed some other means of justifying her position.

Predictably, that produced a bottleneck in productivity where other employees who needed information had to go through her to get it before they could do their jobs. How did this situation arise? Because there wasn't a common trust from the top down focused around a particular goal and thus no sense of unification among team members. Serving only in the interest of not getting fired, this one employee acted in her own self-interest and harmed the entire company as a result.

Leaders at companies where problems like this are an issue will notice right away because balls will get dropped: things will slip through the cracks, deadlines will be missed, and milestones won't be met. Each of these is an inevitable symptom of poor communication and access to information, which are themselves symptoms of a company lacking clearly defined goals.

When there's perfect communication, things like that don't happen unless there's been a natural disaster of some sort that ravages the infrastructure needed to make it possible—and even then, chances are a good team can figure out a way to get things done. If that isn't happening, there's a good chance it's because people are acting in their own interests rather than serving the organization's goal.

The odds of that mentality being in place are particularly high with salespeople, who are often predisposed to rely on their own intuition, instinct, and abilities. It's not uncommon for that tendency to create an environment where asking questions feels like weakness rather than a necessary tool for growth—a dynamic that hinders their personal growth as well as their results. If they aren't naturally closing deals left and right, they can begin to feel that they aren't valuable, especially if any of the glory that comes about when they do close can be attributed to a script rather than their own talent.

The natural result of that is that many become lone wolves, secluded in their offices while the remainder of the team works in a more open environment. Relying on their own skills limits the breadth of knowledge from which they can draw, and it ultimately results in mishandled leads. In the case of the partnership management software company I mentioned earlier, this manifested itself as a singular focus on the product, and before long, their salespeople were listing so many features that their customers didn't even know what was being discussed.

If leads are confused or have questions, it becomes increasingly difficult for them to ask because the salesperson's confidence makes the concepts being discussed seem like basic knowledge. Soon prospects will pretend like they know what's being proposed and then say that it's not a good fit because they don't want to seem like a rube.

That isn't the only way this mentality can cause things to go awry. A salesperson's assumption that they can handle leads on their own might tempt them to email the prospects rather than calling them in the name of saving time. After all, moving thirty leads one step further into the sales process is more efficient than calling four of them, right?

This approach couldn't be further from reality, yet it's often favored over spending time with a smaller selection of leads and truly understanding their needs. Productive conversations—particularly those that follow the connect call—come about when salespeople do in-depth research beforehand, not when they wing it based solely on their ability to communicate. At the end of the day, it's better to have moved a single prospect significantly farther down the sales funnel than to have inched thirty prospects closer, none of whom are significantly more likely to close.

Of course, anyone can tell you that the way people view phone calls in general has shifted in recent years with voice usage dropping as preferences for texting and data rise. Author and marketing expert leader Gary Vaynerchuk attributes this to a fundamental focus on time—primarily in the sense that people don't want to waste it.

Becoming harnessed to a conversation can sometimes feel that way, and if you don't believe that, then you've clearly never been hit up by a telemarketer. Here's the thing: if you're calling people within five minutes of receiving their information, as I have argued you should, and you're helping them with problems they're trying to solve, you aren't wasting anyone's time. At that moment, they aren't doing anything except trying to find answers—they aren't in a meeting or out with their friends, but searching for something that will make their lives easier.

Sure, what you're doing is actually making a well-disguised sales call, but done properly, it will still delight them because it will provide relevant information at the same time.

Developing this mindset was one of the first things we did at the channel relationship management software company where the concept of non-interruptive marketing had been extended to the sales side, causing a gap to form between the two. Salespeople were sending casual emails when a lead came in as opposed to making a phone call because they had overapplied the fundamentals of inbound marketing—they were effectively baiting the fish, but they weren't reeling them in.

You don't have to be the world's most successful bassmaster to know that hooking a fish immediately is always preferable to doing nothing and hoping it will swim a little closer to the boat first. Yet this is the exact mentality companies fall victim to time and time again. If you take nothing else from this book, put this culture change in place: Call every lead within 5 minutes after they convert. You will surpass your competitors, who likely don't realize that effective inbound marketing and sales means you aren't making cold calls anymore—you're making warm ones.

Customers are inviting you to call the second they give you their phone numbers, and they're doing it because they need answers. That means your call will almost certainly be met with gratitude, not the sense of dread that those who don't understand the psychology at play so often expect.

Whether leads are being mishandled because of an aversion to making phone calls or because the salesperson is acting as a lone wolf, these mistakes often happen without conscious awareness on the part of the person making them, which is why it's vital to have a system in place that analyzes how effective every call truly is. Without a form of oversight that can objectively measure a salesperson's in-call performance, the person in charge is essentially taking the salesperson's word as to whether the call went well or not. Despite what we're told by conventional wisdom, perception is not reality when it comes to profitable sales performance.

The stark difference between the two is something I've seen firsthand at Hüify, where we once had a salesperson claim a particular lead was rude to her, when, in actuality, it was the salesperson herself who became defensive and condescending after her lead tactfully pointed out how poorly the call was being handled. Although she truly believed her version of the events, it doesn't change the fact that it didn't match up with how things actually occurred, and that experience was a useful reminder that when salespeople aren't selling your product, they're going to be selling to you the allegedly amazing job they're doing.

In situations like that, it helps to think of your organization as a football team and to communicate to your staff that everyone has to be a top performer if they want to win a Superbowl. If someone falls short, he or she is going to bring the whole team down because others will be taking on the burden of that person's work. Eventually it will become necessary to cut that person, if for no other reason than to benefit the company's culture.

These situations won't always be cut and dry: the person you let go could very well be one of the primary "doers" in the group—someone who's always busy, but never seems to produce actual results. Recently, we had an employee who was the first person in the door in the morning and the last person to leave at night, but was simply unteachable. Even though our team grew fond of this person over time, after we let him go, it seemed every team member had a story about extra work he or she had to do because of that person's poor performance.

Was letting that person go a tough decision? Of course it

was, but by definition, leaders have to make tough decisions on a regular basis, and the faster you do it, the better off your company will be. Far from fostering fear, it provides an opportunity to communicate to those who remain why they are important and point out how valuable it is to have coworkers whose proficiency makes their lives easier. That alone is often enough to shift everyone into a growth-driven mindset where future employees who slow the process are more likely to be ferreted out rather than swept under the rug.

In reality, though, it doesn't have to reach that point. If the Gap is effectively closed, all parties will be cooperating so effortlessly that situations like the one outlined earlier aren't likely to ever arise. A key component of creating that environment is the service level agreement (SLA)—a contract where both the sales and marketing divisions agree to perform a certain degree of service to benefit each other.

Remember, our goal is to remove the individual from the equation and place our focus on the overall success of the company, and there's no better way to do that than by putting what's expected in writing. This should actually be in writing or printed, not a PDF or some other electronic means of reaching an accord. A signed and dated piece of paper communicates accountability, which is what the SLA is really all about.

Once it's in writing, there can be no backtracking or questioning unspoken expectations, which often happens in behind-the-scenes conversations and emails. With an SLA in place, the ground rules are set for both sides to be accountable to one another.

It probably goes without saying that there's a certain degree of fear that comes with signing such an agreement, and it's the same fear that sometimes hampers efforts to implement the other changes discussed in this book: no one wants to admit they've been doing things the wrong way. It seems safer to continue doing things the way they've always been done until there's a mandated change as opposed to being the innovator who takes risks in the name of progress.

Another factor is the increase in transparency that often results from an SLA, which could potentially expose ineffective workers once their data is universally known. As with most fears, all of these are based in emotion and insecurity, not logic and reason, so a smart leader can address them simply by drawing attention back to the goal, which, in this case, is to make the company better. As long as the company can prove it is committed to its employees and value them, many of these fears can be subdued.

So what should the agreement itself look like? Obviously,

that varies based on the priorities of the company where it's being put in place, but at Hüify, we've identified a handful of key concepts that must be included. For the most part, they're centered on things we've already discussed in this book:

- Following up with leads is job number one, and our salespeople do so within five minutes of receiving them.
- Sales has to assume marketing is doing a good job, freeing the marketers themselves up to be less critical of their creative work and to focus more on performance-based results.
- Both parties will provide weekly reports, with sales outlining where various leads are in the queue and marketing detailing incoming lead activity.
- The two divisions will have a monthly meeting to discuss ways to improve communication, whether through something as basic as the creation of streamlined email templates or something as involved as finding a way to get requests out sooner.

We take those active-dialogue concepts and place them into a document. You can see an example of a completed SLA at closingculture.com/sla.[5]

5 Adapted from HubSpot's agency partner resources

In this hypothetical example, we filled in data points based on general Hüify sales and marketing details to show you what a real-world sales agreement might look like. (Note: This is not our actual Hüify SLA data.) You will notice that our example SLA is broken out by channel and personas. Not all leads are created equally, and they will all close at different rates. For example, because they are generally nurtured, your email leads should close faster than those from PPC ads, which simply came from clicking on a single ad. Similarly, different types of target customers will produce different total dollar values per deal.

You could easily create your own SLA right now using a similar template. Our template is also available for you to download at closingculture.com/sla.

This template is designed to help you narrow in on your pipeline numbers and create your own SLA with your sales team. You can accomplish this by following four steps:

1. Define your customer close rates
2. Determine a dollar value for your leads
3. Identify how many monthly leads both sales and marketing need to hit your monthly numbers
4. Tally your monthly productivity against these goals

In order to fill out this template, you should have your

sales and marketing analytics ready to go. Look at your historical marketing performance in Salesforce, or your own CRM application. Also, look at your closing histories to make sure you have a clear picture of how your leads go through your funnel. Most of these insights are available in integrated marketing software platforms such as HubSpot and your sales CRM tools.

Here's a breakdown of each step:

STEP 1

The first step of your sales-marketing SLA is to determine your sales closing rates for each lead source and customer persona. To tease out your overall closing rates percentage, look at your last six months of sales data for each channel that you used to generate marketing leads. In the SLA example sheet, we include several inbound sources including organic, social, email, and PPC, as well as outbound calling. Additionally, we include our three customer personas: small businesses, medium businesses, and enterprise companies. When you move to your SLA worksheet, cover all the different channels and personas to include all your leads. Take the average close rate and add it to the correct cell in the document. Remember to update this spreadsheet every month, as your channel performance will change over time.

STEP 2

The second step is to determine the value of each lead source. Knowing the value of your leads is crucial in evaluating your overall pipeline. If you don't know how much each type of lead is worth, it's impossible to know how to allocate your scarce sales and marketing resources. Knowing the value of your leads is important, and calculating it is simple. First, identify your average sale price for each of your core personas. Again, find this data in your marketing software and sales CRM tools. Your average small business sale may be $500, but a larger enterprise company could be double that number. Input your average sale value into the top "average sale price" row for each persona. Our SLA template will automatically calculate the value of your leads based on the close rates percentage you filled in for step 1. Again, revisit your average sale prices for your personas on a monthly basis to make sure you are holding your team accountable and staying on track.

STEP 3

The third step is to break down your monthly lead generation by channel. By looking at actual monthly data in real time, you can see which channels are performing each month and which need to be corrected to hit your projected numbers. Monthly lead tracking gets the whole team on the same page, offers insight into which strategies are working, and helps pinpoint underperforming channels. The SLA example shows what a sample month's productivity might look like. For even more visibility, update these leads on an ongoing basis. Hüify managers often monitor these numbers daily, and we send the marketing team a daily summary of our month-to-date performance. After you've completed step three, you will see that the template includes an additional row on the right of the persona averages that tallies the total leads your team generates each month. While it's valuable to look at your monthly numbers by each channel, ultimately, your marketing team's total numbers determine their success. This is the statistic you will want to have readily available for your sales conversations.

STEP 4

The final section of our calculator will tally your SLA commitments. As you fill in steps one through three, the SLA calculator will automatically fill in the total SLA fields for each channel and persona. This worksheet will add up your channel and persona SLA, as well as your overall monthly totals. Ultimately, the total monthly SLA you commit to should equal the total potential revenue each lead segment can produce per month. As you fill out your tables each month, the SLA calculator will show how you are tracking toward your monthly SLA goal.

By understanding the actual dollar values for your lead generation efforts, you now know how many leads you need, and which channels and personas those leads should be, in order to reach quota. This eliminates any confusion over what leads your marketing team is responsible for each month and creates alignment between your teams.

Use this SLA as a tool to hold sales accountable for following up with these leads. With this data, your sales team can identify exactly how many times they need to attempt contact with their leads in order to deliver on their numbers. Finally, close the loop in your reporting and build this SLA into your reporting structures. This will ensure that this tool becomes a resource for both marketing and sales teams to measure your mutual success.

If the concepts here sound familiar, that's because the SLA is similar in style to the SMART goals we discussed earlier in this book, which combine to form the backbone of growth-driven decision making. These aren't just the musings of some bored marketer, but a genuine plan for producing unimaginable results: in the past year alone, these tools have helped Hüify reduce its sales cycle from nine months to three weeks, and its revenue has literally quadrupled as a result. By the end of this year, we are projecting even greater growth, and there's a sense that the sky really is the limit when it comes to how well the company can do next year.

Now we want to use technology to help other companies do the same thing, but you have to have the process in mind first. What do you want to accomplish? What areas of your company could really benefit from a standardized, automated system? If you plan on implementing the ideas outlined in this book, which stress instant response above all else, then one of the areas where it's most needed is almost certainly lead notification. As soon as a lead visits your website, you need to have a system in place to give you a notification instantly. At Hüify, we use the HubSpot CRM, which can produce an email alert as well as send a push notification to your smartphone. Our sales team often receives three to four notifications for any given lead, and when they hear that sound, they automatically know what's going on and where they should focus their energy.

If you're not ready to dive into HubSpot, you can start with the freemium tool HubSpot Sales, which allows you to pay based on the number of notifications you receive and works as an email-tracking tool. It's built to notify salespeople when someone opens an email they've sent or clicks on a link inside, and it can be combined with almost any CRM to do the same thing for websites. Imagine the peace of mind that results from being absolutely certain you aren't missing any opportunities—from knowing without a doubt that you will be notified any time there is a new lead. As far as the results go, look no further than the appendix of this book for a peek at what these concepts and systems are already doing for some of our clients.

CONCLUSION

PUTTING IT ALL TOGETHER

As the average customer experience has evolved over the years to keep pace with the changes wrought by the rise of the web, marketing, too, has adapted to the times. The rise of inbound and content marketing are clear indicators that professionals in the field are paying more attention than ever to the buyer's journey.

Sales professionals, on the other hand, seem to be operating on many of the same principles they have had for decades, leading to a stagnant culture that's inherently incompatible with the latest marketing efforts. Often, they see themselves as an organization's maverick gunslingers—a brotherhood unto themselves occupied solely with reaching or exceeding their quotas, even if doing so makes life more difficult for the remainder of the company.

It might seem foolish to think of blowing past sales quotas as a negative occurrence, but it's not hard to imagine a situation where consistently doing so could exceed the organization's capacity to make good on the products or services being sold. After all, only a certain number of widgets can be produced each month, and without proper warning, the operations side of a business could easily be overwhelmed by a massive influx of new deals.

At the opposite end of the spectrum, salespeople often struggle when the leads they're provided are poorly qualified with regard to the likelihood that they'll make a purchase or the degree to which the product or service being sold fits their needs. Their work suffers from a lack of understanding about whom the company wants to do business with and, perhaps more importantly, who is supremely suited to do business with the company.

Unfortunate situations like these are a symptom of a phenomenon we now know as the Gap—a separation between the sales and marketing departments that results in missed opportunities for both.

Above all else, the central thesis of this book is that it's long past time for salespeople to overhaul their culture in a way that stresses communication with marketers and to hone a laser-like focus on continually improving customer experience. From the day they first visit a company's website until they receive their final invoice, sales staffs across the globe should be primarily occupied with ensuring that each step along the way is easy and even pleasurable.

The blueprint for doing so is based on a foundation of prioritizing initial contact with new leads, making it vital that salespeople contact and establish a relationship with them as soon as possible. A company's culture should reflect this fundamental necessity by creating an environment where members of its sales staff are notified of leads as soon as they arrive and are free to pursue them immediately, regardless of whatever internal work they may have been doing at the time.

This culture change could manifest itself in any number of ways: salespeople may have to leave meetings, postpone reports, or make other changes to their workflow to make way for a response time that expresses value for their customers. As we've already determined, it's imperative that a technological infrastructure be in place that allows instantaneous notification of the arrival of leads so a response can occur in five minutes or less.

Implementing CRM software is paramount to this

endeavor, as it creates a central place where a company's marketing and sales staffs can see what kind of communication has taken place with a new lead and, ideally, determine what their interests may be.

Of course, it would be unrealistic to expect a system to run this efficiently if everyone involved in its success is left to operate on his or her own intuition and expectations. There are simply too many opportunities for people to misjudge the quality of a new lead and to prioritize other work over the need to contact that potential customer, particularly if it doing so leads to overtime or additional work.

Combating these natural human instincts is most effective when the staff involved in the process is held to a documented process based on a predetermined goal. Everyone in the company, from the highest-ranking executive to the intern starting her first day of work, needs to be rallied behind a grand, existential vision that is SMART—specific, measurable, attainable, relevant, and timely.

Having that in place helps stave off the urge for people to create their own internal to-do lists and instead refocuses their attention on what will help push the organization toward its ultimate conclusion.

These may seem like common-sense suggestions that

should be in place at any company hoping to become successful, but poor leadership often prevents many of them from taking shape. In dozens of cases, many of which we've detailed in this book, key players in major companies are not only unwilling to disclose the direction their organization is headed, but they're also often completely unaware of it. Instead of discussing grand, overarching visions, they are concerned with hitting a personal quota for new leads or building a marketing department because some industry "expert" said they should.

It's not hard to imagine how much more valuable a meaningful goal would be in terms of motivating these employees. Instead of simply working to hit their quota, workers need to know and be reminded that doing so will help their company expand into the Asian market, hire a new team, or raise a new round of funding.

These kinds of goals can only come from an organization's leadership, who should go out of their way to avoid making workers feel like hamsters running circles on a meaningless wheel. Successful leadership is predicated on giving one's subordinates something to strive for that's bigger and more tangible than an arbitrary number.

In case you're tempted to believe I'm preaching about something I've never dealt with personally, think again.

It wasn't so long ago that I found myself working as part of a four-person team whose "CEO" had no stated ambition beyond the vague promise of "getting more clients." Because of that, the services we offered our clients varied from client to client, which by its very nature precluded the possibility that our company could ever hope to scale up.

That was nearly a decade ago, and the agency is still staffed by four people. They're just four completely different people, because no one wanted to work in an environment so lacking in consistency or purpose. The rest of us simply grew tired of every insignificant distraction preventing a plan from ever taking shape.

By now, you know what a better system looks like, but you may be wondering how to put that knowledge into practice. What you don't know is that you already have that information too.

Simply begin with what we discussed in the very beginning of this book: determine what you want your company to look like and what kind of customers you want to work with. The relative difficulty of this task and the length of time for which you can plan will naturally depend on the industry in which your organization operates, and it can be particularly difficult in the tech space due to the speed with which advances occur. In spite of these challenges, it should be possible to hew together a rough image of the culture, size, and scope you'd like to achieve within a given time frame.

When we started Hüify, we didn't know how much revenue we'd be bringing in at this point, but we did know what kind of culture we wanted, the size of the staff we hoped to build, and whom we wanted to work with. We were then able to work backward from that image and determine the amount of income needed to sustain healthy profit margins while realizing our vision.

So sit down, clear your head and schedule, and take a few hours to figure out exactly what it is you're trying to build. Once you have that, you can begin to look for meaningful milestones on the road to achieving the overarching vision. Although many of these milestones should be quantifiable in terms of revenue, be careful not to discount the value of qualitative ones, which can often be just as important.

For example: Since our initial mission at Hüify was to stop bad marketing, we knew we'd need to build a team of creative innovators. However, it's rare indeed for two people to agree on what constitutes creative innovation, making it impossible to objectively gauge whether we achieved that goal, even if my subjective opinion is that we have.

What isn't subjective is the revenue growth we've seen since assembling the team, which makes that a quantifiable metric by which we can judge the success of our qualitative goal. By applying a similar formula to your unique goals, you'll be able to keep yourself honest in terms of whether you're progressing appropriately and accurately determine whether a strategy change is or is not in order.

Of course, all the goals in the world are worthless without the means to achieve them, which is why the next step in the process is to create the buyer personas described in chapter two. Figure out who your most profitable, enjoyable customers are (and which are easiest to close) and then create a profile you can use to help find more of them.

A side benefit of arming yourself with such information is that you can begin to tailor the services and products your company offers to the anticipated needs of that ideal client. Your process, plans, sales, and communications efforts can all be custom-built to attract and delight precisely the customer you're hoping to do business with.

Does that person like getting cold calls? Probably not, so you know you need to find another means of getting in touch. Does the person like receiving in-depth progress reports on his or her investment? If not, you know you need to pare your reporting down to only that which is supremely relevant.

Keep thinking along these lines and soon your entire company will be ideally suited to do business with exactly the kind of clients you're looking to attract, and they'll love working with your organization because it's literally tailor-made to their needs.

Once you've successfully implemented a culture built around these principles, the final step is to determine what services your organization is best at and which might be better served by outsourcing them to a third party. An organization supremely effective in operations, for example, is probably not staffed with highly effective salespeople or marketers. With that in mind, it can either attempt to make hires that will improve that situation or turn to professionals who understand both to a highly refined degree.

Of course, hiring those workers in-house means figuring out a way to manage them, which is a task that might be difficult for a company already struggling in those areas of its business. Taking into consideration the additional salaries needed to make the positions attractive to effective talent, organizations often discover savings in both time and money by selecting an experienced outside firm with which to partner.

A partner is exactly what CEOs should be looking for when they consider this step. It's vital that the ultimate selection is a companion organization focused on helping both companies grow in the long term rather than just increasing their own revenue in the short term.

When that partnership exists, the results will speak for themselves, as evidenced by the case studies that appear in the appendix to this book.

APPENDIX: PART I

WHAT CULTURAL CHANGE LOOKS LIKE

Imagine a company whose primary product is an editorial and content management platform for journalists. Crafted by experts with years of experience in the trade, its purpose is to eliminate as many boring administrative tasks from the workload as possible and free up more time for creative professionals to do what they do best: interview sources, write compelling stories, and take great photos.

Additionally, the product contains components that limit the possibility for human error to harm a media outlet's bottom line. It categorizes, curates, and maintains a database of all assets relevant to specific advertising clients and ensures that booked ads appear in the publications and on the websites they're supposed to appear in—every time.

The software is so versatile, it automatically makes necessary alterations between products for print and web, checks the names of the people mentioned in stories against a predefined database of newsmakers, and addresses virtually every other issue media professionals face outside of producing their work. It's deployed as a browser-based application that can be used by reporters, photographers, and videographers anywhere they have access to Wi-Fi.

As mentioned, the company was founded by veterans of the news business with nearly a century of experience between them, which is both a blessing and a curse. On one hand, they're extremely well versed in the problems often faced by those in their profession, allowing them to put together a buttoned-up product that solves those problems without a lot of fuss. But like many of the news industry's older guard, they are cautious about the web and unsure of how to navigate the unfamiliar waters of a more interconnected world.

This mindset has posed a problem for the company since its inception, and in more ways than one. In terms of marketing, it prevents the executives in leadership positions from seeing the value in innovating and keeps them focused on traditional marketing tactics. They send direct mail to newspaper companies, purchase display ads in trade publications, and hand over a fortune to alleged experts who claim they can bring in traffic from Google and other search engines via some esoteric form of web magic only IT professionals could possibly hope to comprehend.

Because most of these marketing methods fail to provide any data for the company's salespeople to use when trying to connect with leads, they often fail to close the type of customers the organization hopes to attract. Even worse, they are wasting a great deal of time on leads that were never going to buy anyway. It's precisely this dynamic that prevents the sales and marketing staffs from seeing the value in talking to one another, so they rarely ever do.

Frustrated and looking for an answer, one of them recently stumbled across the concept of inbound marketing and pitched it to his coworkers as a possible cure for some of these corporate ailments. Many of his colleagues agree: they could generate a far greater number of better-qualified leads if they provided content their potential customers might be interested in and used it to start conversations about their product. However, there's a problem: none of them know how to do it, and even if they did, they likely wouldn't have the necessary time.

Still, our intrepid salesperson (let's call him Jim) presses on, hopeful that a little early success might spur the company to arrange its priorities in a way that would allow the sales team more time to pursue the methodology. But what degree of success would be necessary to inspire such a dramatic shift in the organization's attentions? Jim isn't the CEO. In fact, he isn't even a mid-level manager, and he certainly isn't privy to the kind of information he'd need to determine where his company is headed.

If he asked his colleagues, they'd say, "We need more leads." Jim, however, wants a real goal—some tangible cause he can use to rally his coworkers to action. Certainly, his company wants to sell more subscriptions to its service. That is understood, but what are the organization's long-term goals? What kind of revenue does it need to reach them? How much of that extra revenue does the company expect to come from its inbound marketing efforts?

Jim soon realizes he should be able to answer these questions, but beyond the vague notion of "producing more leads," such topics are rarely discussed at his company. At least, they aren't discussed with mere salespeople. Jim decides he needs to bring some of the organization's top executives in on his efforts if he hopes to acquire the kind of goal he'll need to succeed.

Soon he's having dinner with the company's CEO, and it's

during this conversation that he discovers he and his colleagues are actually working for something much bigger than themselves. Over the course of the discussion—aided by the relaxed atmosphere of a pleasant meal—Jim's boss reveals the company's top-level executives have been in acquisition negotiations with some of the country's leading media companies, but they need additional revenue to prove their concept is solid and their organization solvent.

How much revenue? Approximately $500,000 in the next six months.

It might be tempting to think that Jim and his colleagues would be put off by the prospect of acquisition, but the reality of the situation is that everyone involved stands to benefit. The cofounders of the company will be paid handsomely, existing employees will receive bonuses, and the added legitimacy of a major organization will allow the company as a whole to compete for clients at a much higher level. Even if none of those potentialities were factors in the equation, Jim could still use the revenue goal for his original purpose: inspiring the organization to reorganize its marketing efforts in a more effective way.

The only remaining problem is that, although he has a few ideas as to what kind of content will produce the biggest increase in quality leads, Jim has no idea where to start.

The online resources he's gathered offer a plethora of tips, tricks, and techniques designed to achieve the goal he's aiming for, and his colleagues have offered suggestions of their own that seem worthy of exploration. Nevertheless, with so much information on hand, it's difficult to tell which will be most effective with the specific clientele he needs to attract.

Jim decides he needs to test all of the strategies and allow the results to speak for themselves in terms of performance in his market. While he's confident at least some of the strategies will prove successful, he also knows many—perhaps even a majority—will fail. Inevitably, at least one of the team members who suggested a failing strategy will see its failure as a reflection of his or her value to the company. How can Jim keep his coworkers from becoming discouraged and shying away from proposing other ideas that could prove beneficial?

There's really only one way to accomplish this: a cultural shift in which each worker's attachment to individual ideas is diminished while constant innovation and iteration are emphasized. Staff at every level will be encouraged to test preconceived notions about everything and implement policies that the data gained from those experiments suggests are most likely to be effective.

In other words, staff members need permission to fail so that they can ultimately succeed. To facilitate that mentality, Jim decides one of the very first tests will be related to something he has vocally supported since beginning his endeavor: the company's alleged need for a new website. If the data gained from the test proves his theory true, he'll have the evidence he needs to convince his superiors to move forward with the expenditure required to launch a new site. And if the data doesn't support a need for a new site, he can demonstrate firsthand how he wants his coworkers to approach the failure of their own ideas and projects—not with fear or self-loathing, but with excitement at the prospect of learning something new.

It's the second of these possibilities that turns out to be a reality, and the company ultimately ends up simply adding a blogging component to its existing site so as to facilitate the inbound tests. For a fraction of what a full redesign might have cost, they have their landing page retooled to feature the blog more prominently, but keep everything else much the same as it's always been. This way, the organization's existing clients are saved the trouble of learning a new interface—one they may potentially hate—and the company is able to allocate more resources to testing various iterations of its new marketing strategy.

The upgrades that are added all serve a purpose: to convert

potential customers who visit the page into sales leads who can then be closed by people like Jim. There's just one problem. The company doesn't know what kind of customers it really needs to attract. After all, past marketing efforts have essentially been scattershot approaches that attempted to present the company's product as a one-size-fits-all solution to the universal problems that plague every media entity. However, faced with the need to produce content that shares relevant solutions with at least some degree of depth, Jim must learn more about his audience. He needs to connect with them, to understand who they are, and to learn what they're looking for when they come to his company's website.

He may not call them buyer personas, but that's exactly what Jim needs if he hopes to write content that will appeal to the customers who will help the organization reach its goal. To create them, he takes a look at the clients the company is already serving and assesses the commonalities that link those who are the easiest to do business with. Which customers' needs fit the organization's product like a hand fits inside a glove? Who was so hungry for a solution to their problems that they bought in with minimal effort and remained loyal customers ever since?

It isn't long before Jim notices some patterns. Nearly every client who comes to mind while he ponders questions about the company's customer base are young publishers in charge of medium-sized, locally focused media companies. They're dedicated professionals who know they need to move their organizations into the twenty-first century quickly if they hope to survive in the current market, and they are open to innovation. Like most journalists, they consider themselves at work 24-7, and they will require any needed software to work well at any time, or to be serviced promptly when it breaks down.

After reverse engineering this buyer persona from an amalgamation of personality traits exhibited by current clients, Jim can now craft content designed to appeal specifically to those customers, running the gamut from fun compilations of hilarious headlines to serious pieces examining the state of the industry—and everything in between. To ensure that these articles are seen, targeted advertising is used to reach the desired buyer persona on social media apps such as LinkedIn and the websites of industry luminaries.

Of course, not all of these efforts are successful, but when one doesn't produce, the people involved examine it for weaknesses and try something new—just like Jim did when his website experiment came to a close. They test different color schemes in their ads, write blog posts about different topics (or address the old topics in different ways), and continue to iterate until they discover what works.

Every time a potential customer interacts with any of these lures, the company's marketing staff is able to learn about their interests, desires, and behaviors, allowing the company to tailor an email automation workflow to the specific times the users are optimally available. In addition to creating a personalized experience using image and copy variance, this increases click-through rates and minimizes cancellation of subscriptions among the lead base who have provided email addresses to the system.

Using the data harvested from these changes, the company's marketing department is uniquely positioned to provide esoteric insights into each individual lead. That said, the information itself is useless unless put into the hands of a salesperson. The handoff requires a level of communication between the two departments that hasn't previously existed.

In fact, before the push to make these changes began, the departments were housed at separate ends of the company's corporate office and rarely dealt with each other directly. After all, what information could marketing have provided sales that required more than a simple email to communicate? They had been producing little more than names, phone numbers, and email addresses. Now they were amassing in-depth details about their leads' desires, habits, and needs.

It's clear that something has to change, but both sides are replete with proud employees who are hesitant to admit they've been doing things wrong for the past several years. What if they end up getting fired for their lack of foresight? What if having others directly involved in the work they're doing exposes it as being subpar? Fears like these prevent both salespeople and marketers from seeing the benefits of combining their efforts, which impedes the progress needed for the firm to reach its goal.

Fortunately, Jim has the good sense to realize that moving his colleagues past their irrational fears will require shaking up the roles they've created for themselves. In an effort to perform this Herculean feat of psychology, he arranges another dinner—this time with his boss, the head of sales, and the company's chief marketer.

Jim is able to connect with the men on a human level outside of their work environment. He communicates respect for them and their positions while urging them to embrace needed change. By the end of the night, he's demonstrated that his interests lie not in some mutinous plan to usurp the company's leadership, but in pushing the organization toward a mutually beneficial goal.

When they return to work, the heads of both departments are able to rally their teams to the cause. The only remaining doubt is over what new responsibilities will be expected of the employees in each division. Where do marketing efforts end and sales efforts begin? What degree of support does one department need from another in order for both to succeed in this unfamiliar environment? How will both sides know when they're succeeding?

Everyone involved must agree on all of these points if the new regime is to have any hope of measuring its effectiveness and holding itself accountable. By now, they've learned that a centerpiece of their success will be a quick response to incoming leads on behalf of the sales team, so that gets included in the Service Level Agreement that results from these discussions. The importance of universal knowledge regarding both the number of leads coming in and the status of those moving toward the end of the funnel has also been recognized for its value, so sales and marketing are further required to produce periodic reports that speak to both. There are other factors, many of them specific to the industry in which the company operates, which are outlined in the agreement and signed by every member of the team.

Combined with assorted pieces of technology from HubSpot, the accord positions the departments to communicate like never before. The time it takes a salesperson to respond to a new lead drops, while the amount of information the salesperson has about the lead prior to the call skyrockets. Marketing is analyzing and screening leads to ensure that they match up with the company's target buyer persona and ensuring that the sales staff knows which ones are most promising before they ever pick up the phone.

The effects of all this change come about slowly, but after a few months, they've proven unquestionably beneficial. Open and click-through rates on the company's marketing emails have increased exponentially. Whereas their landing page once converted 5–15 percent of the people who visited it, the rate is now moving closer to 80 percent. Most importantly, revenue is up, and it is rapidly approaching the goal determined at the outset of the engagement.

Meanwhile, on the other side of the country, a man named Steve has a problem: the media company he's been charged with guiding into the twenty-first century has grown too large to rely on the systems it's currently using. Where a team of editors, producers, and account executives could once manage every phase of news and advertising production, now there are too many moving parts for them to even effectively oversee operations—critical aspects of the business. Advertising slips through the cracks, news stories are published with errors, and a general decrease in the company's level of professionalism seems imminent.

Steve needs to come up with a solution, and fast. So he turns to the web, where he finds a plethora of articles and blog posts written by people who seem to have dealt with the same issues he's currently facing. One website seems to stand out from the rest, though. While the overall website site is informative and helpful, the articles there hint at some larger, deeper truth that's notably absent in some of the other free material he's seen. So he gives them his contact information in exchange for access to something more substantial.

Before Steve has a chance to delve into that new information, however, his phone rings. On the other end of the line is a man named Jim, who seems to know an awful lot about both Steve's company and the dilemmas it's presently facing.

In fact, it isn't long before Steve realizes Jim may have just the answer he's looking for.

APPENDIX: PART II

REAL-LIFE EXAMPLES

BRIDGING SALES AND MARKETING—A CASE STUDY ON CAP3

Due to CAP3's growth, the company was looking for a way to scale past its owner acting as the primary salesperson and building a strategy that would allow for other sales people to further the process. Hüify helped create a sales procedure, a lead nurturing structure, and an effective way to hand off leads from marketing to sales.

CAP3 currently has an inbound lead follow-up response time of less than five minutes. Sales development training system specific to CAP3's business is beginning to take shape, and there is a clear service level agreement (SLA) that exists between marketing and sales.

THE CAP3 STORY—YOUR LOYAL VIRTUAL ACCOUNTING TEAM

CAP3 provides businesses with leadership, direction, and a full team for all things accounting. CAP3 operates virtually and functions primarily as a firm's accounting department.

THEIR GOAL FOR HÜIFY—THE HANDOFF

Build a streamlined handoff process where the leads brought in through Hüify's marketing process are transitioned seamlessly, at scale, and as efficiently as possible. Additionally, Hüify sought to align the cultures between both sales and marketing.

THEIR SOLUTION—LESS THAN FIVE MINUTES

Since a majority of CAP3's inbound leads were from referrals, we knew that it was critical that they responded as quickly as possible. Everyone decided that a response time of less than five minutes was required. This almost immediate follow-up would communicate value and structure to an incoming lead. Coupled with CAP3's reputation, this strategy would help the company close a lot more business.

Products Used

- HubSpot Sales
- HubSpot CRM

Goals

- Build a scalable handoff process from marketing to sales
- Align the "closing culture" of marketing and sales
- Reach an average of less-than-five-minutes response time for inbound leads

THEIR SUCCESS—A FLAWLESS TRANSITION

The handoff and closing culture implemented by Hüify resulted in the following:

- Culture change from a lifestyle to a high-growth organization
- Structured sales process foundation that the company will be able to scale with
- Great peace of mind for leadership because each step is clearly defined and everyone knows what needs to happen next

As a result of these changes, CAP3 will become one of the fastest growing accounting firms on the East Coast. Observe this growth with us or even be a part of it by checking out their website: www.gocap3.com.

SAAS COMPANY—SALES FUNNEL ADVISING AND SETUP

During their annual promotion at the beginning of 2015, this SaaS company company drove 200 new leads. The following year they worked with Hüify to strengthen their funnel in the months leading up to the annual promotion. The area that needed the most attention was the connection between marketing and sales. The sales team was not on the same page with marketing and new sales opportunities would fall through the cracks. On top of lost revenue from neglected leads, their retention rate suffered due to this disconnect between departments. Before we could focus on bringing in new leads, the following culture issues were addressed in the months leading up to their annual promotion:

- Marketing and Sales handoff issues were mitigated by creating a SLA
- An optimized funnel and sales process were implemented which drastically decreased the number of leads slipping through the cracks
- Their HubSpot portal was overhauled, cleaned up, and connected with their existing technology, which added even more accountability between Sales and Marketing by connecting all platforms and data that both departments were using
- Sales and Marketing communication in general was improved by aligning both team around SMART goals

THEIR GOAL—INCREASE LEADS AND REVENUE FROM THE ANNUAL PROMOTION

In previous years, the SaaS Company would average 200 leads from their 30-day annual promotion at the beginning of the year, with around 15% of these leads becoming customers. And and although their close rate was relatively high, they struggled to retain these customers in the months after the promotion.

One of the SMART goals we set was to gain more than 400 new demo requests during the 30-day annual promotion— a 100% increase from the year before. Both Hüify and the SaaS Company's internal team were excited, but appropriately nervous as an ambitious growth goal had been set.

THE SOLUTION—INCREASE CONVERSIONS AND CLOSE THE LOOP

Our teams started by focusing on the visit-to-lead conversion process. We decreased the amount of steps a website visitor had to complete to become a lead on the site while also increasing the reasons why someone might want to convert by articulating the value of the promotion more clearly and directly on our pages and other marketing assets. Workflows were put into place to nurture unqualified leads who only completed the first step in the demo request process by reminding them via email about how this promotion could change their business. Workflows were also set up to automatically email those demo request leads that had completed the process and invite them to access their demo.

Products Used

- HubSpot CRM
- HubSpot Sales: Letting the sales team know when their emails were being opened
- HubSpot CMS: New Landing Pages that were better optimized for the visitor
- HubSpot Automated Workflows and Emails

Goals

- Unite the UK and US Sales teams with Marketing
- Gain more than 400 new demo requests during a 30-day annual promotion period
- Increase the visit-to-lead conversion rate for the website

THEIR SUCCESS—2X GROWTH IN LEADS AND REVENUE

Hüify was able to design an easier conversion path for the website visitors. By creating more accessible places to enter their information, as well as making the landing pages more clear in the benefit the SaaS Company provides, the leads poured in from the site traffic. Over 450 leads converted on the site and were nurtured by the company's inside sales team. They converted 20% of those leads into customers. The key efforts that helped drive this success were:

- Making the website copy more articulate and clear regarding the value that could be provided to the visitor
- Creating better landing page layouts that invited the web traffic to absorb the new information
- Set up the technology and trained the sales team to make sure they could connect with a lead as soon as possible
- Created email workflows that guaranteed immediate contact with the sales team

Because of this growth, this company was able to successfully meet their hiring and expansion goals. Their customer base became more reliable and diversified between the two countries.

The case studies presented in this section illustrate the kind of results that companies can attain when they enjoy the strong sense of purpose that comes from having clearly stated goals and a measurable plan for how to reach them. In each case, Hüify's process provided the missing processes that were needed to propel the companies in question to new heights, and we did so by focusing on each organization's culture.

From a leadership perspective, we kept the focus on the stated goals and rallied the teams that had been assembled to continuously push toward that conclusion. It would have been easy for those involved to start pointing fingers when things didn't work the right way rather than contributing to the solution, but that didn't happen because they were continually reminded about what was going to drive the whole company forward. Once they were aligned behind that cause and rallied around each other, the next step was to facilitate growth-driven decision making as a tool for developing an iterative mindset.

That alone allowed us to diminish opportunity costs to such a degree that the usual concerns about developing a new marketing strategy—how long it will take and how much it will cost before it gains traction—became a nonissue. We were researching; building buyer personas; creating new websites, and performing hundreds of tiny, incremental tests all at the same time, which allowed us to show results early and often.

That kind of environment allows the team to quickly adapt

to changing circumstances and, perhaps more importantly, make short wins that provide periodic boosts to morale. Instead of working through roadblock after roadblock toward a goal that was months away from being realized, everyone involved was able to see real progress on a near-daily basis, encouraging each person to give his or her best effort.

Adopting a growth-driven mindset also weeds out the unqualified opinions of the people involved and replaces them with only those concepts that are supported by research and data. Our team came to an agreement on what would be tested, and as noted earlier, outperformers always won. As for the ideas that failed, those who dreamed them up still received the validation of having their concepts tested, and no one ridiculed them when things didn't pan out as they'd hoped. Instead, everyone involved was simply grateful for the knowledge gained from the outcome of the test.

This book has given you the tools you need to create results just like these: a means of creating a true understanding of your goals, a method for creating buy-in to those goals, a guide on focusing your team on results, and a template for the agreement needed to make your marketing and sales staffs work as one. So what are you waiting for? There are clients out there who want exactly what you have.

I hope you have enjoyed this book, and that the information contained in it transforms your business the same way it has many other companies. If you would like to connect, you are more than welcome to email me: josh@huify.com. Or you can follow me on any social platform of your choosing (username: JoshHarcus). Suggestion: For the best "behind the scenes" look at my life connect with me on Snapchat http://huify.co/SnapJosh (case sensitive).

Happy closing.

ABOUT THE AUTHOR

JOSH HARCUS is the founder and CEO of Hüify, an inbound marketing and sales agency. After observing the profound negative impact on revenue that disjointed sales and marketing teams create, Josh created an agency that did away with the practice of using the fluffy vanity metrics as a means for indicating success. Instead, Josh and his team focus on genuine, measurable, and attainable outcomes that help take Hüify's clients beyond the stagnating threshold of mediocrity and into new levels of success for their brand.

Josh has consulted brands such as Car and Driver, Springer Global Publishing, HubSpot, and SureScripts. He has also spoken alongside Google, Facebook, Bing, and HubSpot, and at conferences such as INBOUND.

59225294R00097

Made in the USA
Charleston, SC
31 July 2016